12 Week[illegible] Sober Life

12 Weeks To A Sober Life

A Guided Gratitude Journal For
Daily Progress Towards Your Sober Self

JOHN RISBY

With a foreword by Sarah Woods
Edited by Chris Humphreys

12 Weeks To A Sober Life

Published by Alcohol-Free Press

Alcohol-Free Press is an imprint of
The Mindful Drinking Company Limited
Commerce House, Carlton Boulevard, Lincoln LN2 4WJ

www.alcoholfree.press
info@alcoholfree.press

ISBN: 978-1-9168962-0-8

Disclaimer: Neither the author nor the publishers are medical experts. Advice given in this book is based on many years of personal experience and interaction with other people recovering from alcohol use disorders. If you are concerned about your drinking you should always seek a medical opinion from your doctor. Stopping drinking abruptly can be dangerous for some people and neither the author nor publisher can take any responsibility for any consequence of your actions while attempting to stop or reduce your drinking.

For my beautiful, kind, clever, funny, generous, witty, and generally wonderful daughter Julia Marie Risby Fernández, who continues to amaze me every single day.

I hoped for a miracle when I stopped drinking, but I never expected one like this.

You have made every step of my journey worthwhile.

I've not always had a "gratitude attitude". But when life began again for me on January 23rd 2008 I knew I needed a mental gear shift.

After two decades struggling with alcohol addiction, I had finally quit drinking – for good. Alcohol had dominated my life and as I faced life without it, I felt elated, excited and utterly daunted all in one.

I had an emotional hill to climb. Why? Well because, for me, staying sober required more than just the act of abstinence. Not putting the glass to my lips was just a part of my life's journey. The rest was re-wiring my mind.

Whilst I was drinking, my thoughts had been as chaotic as my life had become and I'd grown comfy with negative feelings.

Remorse, scorn, shame, anxiety, fear and feelings of utter worthlessness had been constant companions.

To be alcohol-free forever, I needed to fill my life with better vibes and achieve clarity, calm and self-care.

A friend suggested keeping a gratitude journal as a simple, easy way to develop gratefulness – and within a few days I could feel it hot-wiring my brain.

By jotting down the stuff that made me thankful, I gave prominence to the joys of life, and acknowledged positive emotions. So simple!

Few tools have been as beneficial in my AF life as developing an attitude of gratitude.

John's 12 *Weeks to a Sober Life* provides everything you need for the early stages of developing a fresh mindset of thankfulness, from daily incentives, tips and goals, to encouragement, and forward planning.

Each inviting page begs daily discovery – I particularly enjoy the opportunity to review and reflect. Writing daily is also beneficial to me as personally I find it more effective.

If I'm rushed for time in the mornings, I do it before I hit the sack – but on a perfect day I relish time with my journal over breakfast.

Starting the day with a burst of positive thought reminds me, as corny as it sounds, of why it's so good to be alive – and sober.

My lists vary in length as I aim for depth over breadth and I accept that there may be days when I need to gift myself understanding and flexibility.

Some entries are simple, "I'm grateful for the rain.", while others are more elaborate, "I'm grateful for the guy in a transit van who waved me through the traffic safely after an accident shut the A14 - he literally saved me being stuck in a gridlock jam for the entire afternoon." I find good things even on the crappiest of days. Trust me, they are there.

I have learned to be as specific as possible as, for me, specificity fosters a deeper gratitude.

For example, "I'm grateful for my daughter." works. But, "I'm grateful for my daughter who, despite having 'flu herself, brought me a cup of hot lemon in bed when she realised just how lousy I felt." is more effective.

Detailing acts, words, behaviours and natural wonders carries more benefits, I find, than a long, superficial list of products, items and things, so I avoid too much tech and "stuff". It works for me.

In the early days, I used to repeat a lot of the same things each day. I do this less now - although my strong, home-ground Colombian coffee beans still get multiple mentions - as I have learned to zero in on different aspects.

Every week brings new surprises and deeper levels of gratitude and I'm constantly wowed by the many ways the simplest things can bring me joy.

When I managed to get a seat on the bus, I journaled it. When I had the time to read the Sunday newspapers cover to cover, I journaled it. Hearing melodic birdsong and seeing the familiar beaming smile of my best friend all made it onto my list.

Last week I ate a peach when the flesh had reached that sweet spot between soft, juicy and firm. Yep, it's in the journal.

John is no ordinary author for he has developed 12 *Weeks To A Sober Life* through his own experiences with alcoholism.

Like me, John found that a gratitude attitude not only highlights the good things in your life, but also helps prepare and strengthen you to deal with rough patches.

I value that each and every page has been beautifully conceived by someone who has shared my struggles.

As co-founder of the *Alcohol-free Community*, John has also seen gratitude work its magic in a membership that reflects all walks of life.

No matter how difficult and defeating life has felt sometimes, I have always - always - found something to be grateful for. Writing a gratitude journal has had a profound impact on my perspective: I liken it to seeing the world in sunny technicolour now where it once seemed draped in dreary heavy cloud. Dark skies have become brighter. My life has become bigger. My heart more full. My mind less cluttered. My sleep more restful.

In short, through gratitude I have found greater peacefulness, happiness and joy.

I am certain 12 *Weeks To A Sober Life* can do the same for you.

So, I wish you well on your gratitude journey, whether you write your journal at daybreak, on a busy commuter train or just before your turn in for the night.

What's important is the act of appreciating goodness and cementing it into your life so that you too have a "gratitude attitude".

Sarah Woods: *Award-winning Travel Author, Writer & Broadcaster, May 2021*

Sarah

"The availability of good medical care tends to vary inversely with the need for it in the population served."

Julian Tudor-Hart

Giving up alcohol is dangerous, right?

This is something I read a lot on the *Alcohol-Free Community* when people are asking about stopping.

Someone will reply that they shouldn't stop without a medical detox because they could die. Others will reply that they were heavy drinkers but managed to quit successfully without one.

So, what's the truth?

Well, alcohol is an incredibly powerful and dangerous drug. For some heavy drinkers stopping abruptly can cause seizures and other severe reactions. In a very small number of people, this can lead to death.

But this is a very black and white view – the reality is not as stark.

According to the current guidance from the UK's health service advisory board NICE, anyone drinking over 30 units of alcohol a day should undergo detox in a supervised setting, such as hospital, and anyone drinking more than 15 units a day should be offered community support, such as a supervised home detoxification.

However, the NICE guidelines describe best practice, and in an ideal world anyone who wanted to stop would get help the very same day they asked for it.

The sad reality is alcohol and drug services are massively underfunded in the UK and many other countries. People can sometimes be forced to wait months for a medical detox. And those months between deciding to ask for help and getting it can be crucial.

In a properly designed and funded system anyone who sought help would get it immediately but that isn't reality.

And, like most health issues, the Covid-19 pandemic has understandably made the situation worse.

There are different types of drinkers, and different types of drink problems. Not everyone who wants to quit alcohol drinks every day.

Most people who give up drinking are not eating their morning cornflakes with whiskey instead of milk (although I did once know someone who did that).

If alcohol is affecting your life and you want to stop, but you don't drink daily, you are highly unlikely to suffer physical withdrawal symptoms.

Unless you have a serious pre-existing health condition, simply stopping drinking should be perfectly fine on a physical level.

Yours will be more of a psychological battle than physical.

But if you're a daily drinker, and if you drink around 15 or more units a day, you are likely to suffer some form of withdrawal symptoms.

These can include sweating, shaking, and feeling sick and anxious. These will normally last around a week and can be pretty tough.

If you drink over 30 units a day, a self-managed detox is still possible and many people manage it, but it's more important to prepare for your recovery and to gradually reduce your alcohol intake.

Do seek medical help and if you can get a medical detox, that is always the preferred solution.

But experts warn that faced with delays in getting medical help, people will continue drinking. And if that help takes months or even longer, in many cases this is likely to be as, or even more, harmful than a self-detox.

Scottish Health Action On Alcohol Problems (SHAAP) published a DIY guide to self-detoxing in 2020, updated to take into account the effects of the pandemic.

The guide explains the risks of giving up alcohol if you are a heavy drinker, and provides help and information on how to keep a drinks diary and reduce your alcohol intake over the period of a week or so.

It's important to plan carefully and make sure you have support from friends or family.

The main points of the SHAAP guidance are:

- Start a diary to record what you are drinking and how you are feeling
- Keep monitoring your drinking for at least three and up to seven days
- Tell someone you trust of your findings and that you plan to stop
- After three days to a week, begin to reduce your daily unit total
- If you develop severe withdrawal symptoms, contact your doctor

Severe withdrawal can include delirium tremens (DTs) which may result in severe confusion, disorientation, hallucinations, shivering, shaking, sweating and an irregular heart beat.

The guidance also recommends that people seek out support from organisations such as AA who have now made their meetings available online.

Do be careful – but don't use excuses

My own personal experience was one of going cold-turkey as a heavy drinker, and I know many others who did the same. It's not pleasant – in fact, it was down-right horrible. The first few days, and nights in particular, were terrible.

But, with the support of my family and armed with as much knowledge as I could gather, I managed to get through that first week of hell and very quickly things began to improve. So much so, I was able to get to see James Brown live in concert just a week later and actually enjoy myself (probably more so than I would have had I still been drinking).

So yes, while going cold-turkey can be dangerous for some, many experts believe the risk of serious harm is overplayed, and the consequences of not stopping until help is available is understated.

Be careful, be safe, seek medical help if you believe you need it, but use your own judgement and don't use a delay in professional help to put off your recovery.

You can download the SHAAP DIY guide to detoxing from the *Alcohol-Free Community* web site at www.alcoholfree.co.uk/community/diy/

"Failure is instructive.
The person who really thinks
learns quite as much from his
failures as from his
successes."

John Dewey

That first, wonderful, sip...

I started drinking when I was around 13 and from the first sip I knew my life was going to change.

Of course, I thought it would change for the better, and yes, there were good times. If there weren't, who would ever drink enough to develop a problem? But when the problems do develop, they can sneak up on you with little warning.

I remember as time went on going from thinking everything was ok, to thinking maybe it isn't, to knowing it isn't, and from 'no-one else knows' to the horror that, actually, lots of people must know.

Many of us, before we realised we had a problem, knew others with a problem and we'd talk about it or make a joke; Often over a pint...

Things like: 'Yeah, he says he'll do that now. Let's see if he remembers in the morning.' or: 'No, don't ask X, he'll just let us down.' etc.

Realising I had become the person we used to laugh at was like one of those dreams where you're back in school and suddenly realise you're naked. Forgetting to bring years-long overdue homework is optional!

You can try to lie to yourself, but after a while you realise that's not going to work. Then you try to drink your way out of it... great plan John!

And like a baby playing peekaboo, you can think no one knows you're pissed all the time if you don't look at them, so you start hiding away. Of course that doesn't work either. When you look like crap, stink of booze and your life starts falling apart around you, people tend to notice these things no matter how much you try to hide it.

Oh, and when your wheelie bin sounds like a milk float in an accident as you ever-so-slowly and carefully try to take it to the kerb without falling over pissed – that's a good clue too.

Making the decision

It was in 2004 that I finally admitted I was loosing my fight with alcohol. I'd tried to quit a few times before my final, and so-far successful, attempt. The problem was, each time I did, I replaced the booze with another drug.

It was only cannabis – something I'd long given up using in my late teens – but the addict in me meant I used so much I was probably less functional than when I was drinking.

Granted, I didn't argue with my wife as much but only because I was too comatose. I always ended up back on the booze, and each time I returned, the problems became worse.

Eventually, one morning, as I stood in the bathroom running my hands under the cold water in an attempt to cool my overworked liver, I looked at myself in the mirror and didn't recognise the person looking back.

He was a pale, gaunt, sick old man with skin like one of the old codgers from the vault. I was in my early 30s and had always taken care of my skin to an almost compulsive level.

No, something was clearly wrong with that mirror...

Oh course, there was nothing faulty about the mirror at all. It was me that was broken. I had allowed myself to sink to a level that I never dreamt possible. And, despite the attempts at stopping before, I hadn't noticed just how low I had sunk.

Thankfully, that was the wake-up call I needed. I immediately looked up the telephone number for AA and called the helpline. A few hours later I was at my first meeting, and two days later I had my last drink. That was 17 years ago.

I didn't continue with AA past the first year. In the end I decided it wasn't for me, but I will always be eternally grateful for the help and support I received in those rooms and have no hesitation in recommending people try it if they feel they need that level of help.

One of the points of AA is that you get help and you give help in return. That can work from day one – new attendees help remind old-timers of why they are there.

It's also expected that long-term you'll be able to help newcomers with your experience. That's the unwritten deal and, to an extent, when I stopped going to AA, I did feel bad about that. But I found my own path, and my own way to help people.

My own way to give back

In 2006 I co-founded *The Alcohol-Free Shop* with my then-wife – and still friend and business partner – Christine Humphreys. Over the fifteen years since, we've helped countless people with support and advice. Even when that meant telling people who weren't mentally ready for alcohol-free drinks – which can contain up to 0.5% alcohol-by-volume – not to buy from us.

We've never run the business on the basis of screwing people over. In fact, if we ever screwed anyone over, it was ourselves!

We started selling alcohol-free drinks at a time when most people, and certainly most of the drinks industry, found it laughable. But we continued, knowing we were doing the right thing and helping people. Thankfully society seems to be finally catching up with us and alcohol-free drinks are much more common.

But, sadly, there are still many people who suffer from alcohol problems.

In fact, as I finish this book, the news has just broken that in 2020, during the first year of the Coronavirus pandemic, there was a huge increase in the number of alcohol-related deaths in the UK.

Enter the Community

We continue on our journey to try to help people both with *The Alcohol-Free Shop* and more recently with the *Alcohol-Free Community*, which we launched in April 2020 during the first Coronavirus lockdown.

The Community is part of the main web site at www.alcoholfree.co.uk/community/ and we also run a free, private, and confidential group on Facebook that helps people with their drinking.

It's there for anyone who has a concern, whether they want to moderate their intake, whether they know they need to completely stop, or whether they want help staying sober.

It's a wonderful community and, like all communities, it is a sum of its members. Nothing more, nothing less. We may "run" it, but it's the members who make it the wonderful place it is.

If you are looking for a non-judgemental group of people to help you on your journey – whatever your aims are – you couldn't find a more lovely group of people to be by your side.

About journaling

When I stopped drinking in 2004 I didn't journal my recovery, and that's something I regret. It wasn't something that was even on my radar back then.

I did read a lot of other people's experiences, which helped massively, and is something I would encourage everyone to do. And later on, when I went public with my recovery, I started writing articles. But that was about nine years later.

Before then I was too worried what people might think if I came out as a sober alcoholic, so I only told a small number of people and some customers who needed help.

Coming out as a sober alcoholic is a decision everyone has to make for themselves of course, and I know many who keep it quiet – for various reasons – and that's totally their right.

But for me, in the end, it seemed a selfish act – especially as I was running *The Alcohol-Free Shop*. I decided I could do more to help people if I was open and honest.

Since learning about journaling I have no doubt my first year sober would have been easier had I done it. And, from my point of view now, I would have had something I could look back on to see just how I felt every single day of my initial recovery.

When I think back on my recovery now, I feel that – apart from the fact something inside had clearly clicked and I had an utter determination that this time it was going to work – in a way I winged it.

I didn't work the steps when I went to AA. I didn't journal. I didn't know about triggers. I didn't make a gratitude list. In fact, in many ways it's a surprise I managed to make it at all.

It probably took me several years to get to the point that you can get to much sooner by journaling your recovery. I have to hope that, at 17 years sober, I've now caught up on a lot of those things though. Better late than never, yes, but better sooner than later as well. You have the chance here to do it better than I did, I hope you take it.

As an aside, I have to admit to having just taken a few minutes out after writing that last paragraph to wonder at how so many years have gone by so quickly and how different things would have been had I not stopped drinking when I did.

It's impossible to say for sure, but I highly doubt I would be alive right now if I had carried on down the path I was on. I may have been sober for a long time, but I'm not perfect, far – far – from it in fact. I'm not even the best version of me I could be. At least I hope not, I still hope to continue growing and maturing even now as I approach 50.

But, for all my faults, I know I am a million miles away from the broken person who looked in the perfectly functioning mirror that June morning back in 2004 and decided to make a big change.

Please get in touch

I sincerely hope you find this book useful in your goals and welcome all feedback to john@alcoholfree.co.uk (use the subject line 12 *Weeks To A Sober Life* please).

I will personally read all emails and I will reply where appropriate and possible. But, better than talking just to me, join the *Alcohol-Free Community* and talk to a wonderful group of people who are all on a similar path.

Remember, it's never too late to change your life. I, like many others, am living proof of that.

With love and best wishes for your sober life,

John

To accompany this book, I've put together a short series of videos with hints and tips that you can watch as you complete each stage of your journey.

You can view the videos on a special section of our web site just for readers of this book. You can access them at:

www.alcoholfree.press/12weeksbonus

You'll need to enter a secret code to access the web site and then simply enter your email address (don't worry, you won't receive any spam and you can unsubscribe at any time). You'll then receive the videos in your inbox at each stage of your journey.

The secret code is the first word of day 13's tip. Sneak ahead and get the code now then visit the site to sign up and see the videos!

In the morning...

Start every day by writing down three or more things you are grateful for in the heart-shaped balloons. If you want to write more, there is space below.

Next, re-affirm what you will and won't do today in the space provided. Decide how you will reward yourself for a job well done and put that in the treat box.

It's up to you whether this is a daily treat, a weekly treat, or something for the end of the first week or month. You can treat yourself as often and as much as you want!

Write down your goal every morning – even if it's the same every day – and your reward, to remind yourself to keep sight of the prize!

In the evening...

At the end of the day, complete the rest of the page.

Write down what you've learned about yourself and your drinking.

In the smile section, write down one thing that really made you smile. It may be something big, or something small. As long as it lifted your day, write it down! It's important we recognise even the smallest events that improve our lives.

Feel free to doodle and colour the "I have completed day..." section. Colouring – yes, like you did when you were a kid – is a great way to relax and unwind at the end of the day.

Finally, try to go to bed a bit earlier – even if it's just fifteen minutes – to give yourself time to write down your plans for tomorrow.

Then, get a good night's sleep!

MOST OF ALL – BE POSITIVE, <u>YOU CAN DO THIS! xx</u>

"In any given moment we have two options: To step forward into growth or to step back into safety."

Abraham Maslow

Congratulations on starting a journey to a new and better life!

Giving up alcohol can be scary. It can often feel easier to keep things as they are – or, at least, try to. But for many people things will only become worse over time.

The fact you're holding this book in your hands right now is a sign of your commitment to improve your life and, maybe, the lives of those around you.

Regardless of how you feel about yourself right now, you should be proud that you've taken this step. This step alone shows you're prepared to change what you are and where you are.

Giving up alcohol may be one of the biggest decisions you have ever made in your life. It may also be one of the hardest – and the most rewarding.

There's no "one-size-fits-all" solution to stopping drinking. No one can tell you exactly how you will feel. No one can tell you exactly when you will feel better. Your experience is unique.

But the experiences of many people who have made this change already are still valuable and you can use them as a guide for your own journey.

Those who've travelled it before will happily give advice and tips. In fact, for many of us it feels like an obligation to help. An obligation done with pleasure.

There's a whole world out there. It's just waiting for you to discover it. The sea may be choppy at first, but the waters will calm.

Trust me, the journey is worth it.

And as for the destination, where would your dreams take you..?

ARE YOU READY FOR CHANGE? LET'S BEGIN! xx

Don't forget! If you haven't already signed up for the videos, do it now.

DAY 1

Today I am grateful for...

Today I...

Will...

Won't...

I will treat myself to...

Date: __________

Tip for the day

> If you drink over 30 units a day speak to your doctor or an alcohol service before stopping abruptly. It can be dangerous to go cold-turkey. That said, most people – even heavy drinkers – can stop without medical support if you are careful. But make sure you tell someone you are stopping and check in with each other each day – just to say you're OK. Over 15 units a day and you are likely to suffer withdrawal symptoms. Seek medical help if you feel particularly bad. Don't try to quit alone.

Today I learned...

Today I smiled because...

I have completed day...

1

Tomorrow I will...

DAY 2

Today I am grateful for...

Today I...

Will...

Won't...

I will treat myself to...

Date: __________

Tip for the day

"You might have restless nights and stomach cramps for the first few days. Try drinking hot chocolate to sooth your stomach, and consider valerian root (tea or capsules) as a natural sleep remedy.

You can also look at taking other natural remedies such as Milk Thistle to help your liver recover."

Today I learned...

Today I smiled because...

I have completed day...

Tomorrow I will...

DAY 3

Today I am grateful for...

Today I...

Will...

Won't...

I will treat myself to...

Date: ___________

Tip for the day

> It may sound obvious, and it is, but if you don't have alcohol in the house you can't drink it! If you find yourself considering a drink, the extra effort of having to go to the shop will give you time to reconsider.
>
> If you live with other people who drink, ask them to support you by not having alcohol in the house and not drinking in front of you, at least during the early days.

Today I learned...

Today I smiled because...

I have completed day...

3

Tomorrow I will...

DAY 4

Today I am grateful for...

Today I...

Will...

Won't...

I will treat myself to...

Date: __________

Tip for the day

When you stop drinking it's normal for your body to crave sugar. You've been used to getting a lot of sugar from your drinks. You may find you want to eat more sweets and other sugary snacks.

Don't deny yourself – just go for it and eat them. You need to be kind to yourself. Yes, you may put on a few pounds but you can deal with that later – right now you have a more important goal.

Today I learned...

Today I smiled because...

I have completed day...

4

Tomorrow I will...

DAY 5

Today I am grateful for...

Today I...

Will...

Won't...

I will treat myself to...

Date: ___________

Tip for the day

"You've probably been used to drinking a lot of liquids and it's hard to break that habit overnight. Water is a great healthy replacement but some people find it too boring. Alcohol-free wines, beers and other adult alternatives work for many – they also help keep you hydrated.
Others prefer the mental break from anything that looks or tastes similar to alcohol. Only you can decide how you feel on this one. Always err on the side of caution. If you're unsure, don't do it."

Today I learned...

Today I smiled because...

I have completed day...

5

Tomorrow I will...

DAY 6

Today I am grateful for...

Today I...

Will...

Won't...

I will treat myself to...

Date: _________

Tip for the day

"Think about when you normally take your first drink of the day and try to change your routine around this time. This could be as simple as not going to the pub after work, or taking up a new hobby that keeps you busy in the evenings. Anything sport and fitness related is a good option – you avoid the booze and improve your health at the same time! But be careful – if you aren't used to exercise, speak to your doctor first."

Today I learned...

Today I smiled because...

I have completed day...

6

Tomorrow I will...

DAY 7

Today I am grateful for...

Today I...

Will...

Won't...

I will treat myself to...

Date: __________

Tip for the day

"Most people have triggers that cause them to want a drink. It could be work stress, children, watching sport on tv, politics, the news... frankly it can be anything.

Take this time to try to learn your triggers. Write them down when you realise what they are and then work on other ways to cope with the trigger rather than drinking."

Today I learned...

Today I smiled because...

I have completed day...

7

Tomorrow I will...

Week 1 In Review

Date: __________

Things that have gone well...

Things that could have been better...

Things I learned about myself...

Next week I will...

Well done on completing week one!

The first week can be very hard for some people. You should be incredibly proud of yourself for making it this far. If you haven't managed to stay sober each day, don't feel too bad – keep trying and you will get there in the end!

Depending on your level of drinking you may have slept badly and had some odd nightmares! It can be worrying and unpleasant, but it's all very normal. If you've managed to avoid that, be grateful and put it on your gratitude list!

By now though, most people will be past that stage. Going forward your sleep should start to improve. It's different for everyone, of course, so don't worry too much if you don't see an immediate improvement. Don't forget to try hot chocolate, relaxing baths, valerian root or other natural remedies to help you sleep. If you remain concerned, speak to your doctor.

Preparing yourself for week two

The first week may have passed-by in a bit of a blur and you've possibly not been feeling particularly clear-headed. That's normal. Over the following weeks you should regain some mental clarity and now is the time to really start taking advantage of the daily journaling.

Now you've got past this first week of fighting daily battles, you may start to notice certain things – feelings, situations, people, even – that make you want to drink. These are what we call triggers. Everyone has different triggers and it's important you write yours down and reflect on them.

But don't just focus on the trigger itself, dig deeper. Identifying the trigger alone is a bit like taking a painkiller. It's better than nothing and can help for a while, but if you don't find the cause of the pain you'll have to keep taking the tablets.

Examine your triggers closely and see what lies beneath them. You may find that the root cause is actually something very different from what you first thought.

BRING ON WEEK TWO – <u>YOU'RE DOING GREAT!</u>

DAY 8

Today I am grateful for...

Today I...

Will...

Won't...

I will treat myself to...

Date: __________

Tip for the day

A lot of people buy alcohol each day on the way home from work. If you do this, start taking a different route home if you drive, or if you use public transport, maybe get off at a different stop and walk a bit – as long as you aren't going to go past even more booze shops than normal!

If you normally buy booze when you shop for food, go shopping earlier in the morning when you are less likely to buy any alcohol.

Today I learned...

Today I smiled because...

I have completed day...

8

Tomorrow I will...

DAY 9

Today I am grateful for...

Today I...

Will...

Won't...

I will treat myself to...

Date: _________

Tip for the day

"Don't stop drinking for other people, stop for yourself.

Other people will benefit from your sobriety – your partner, children, friends, work colleagues etc – but don't do it for them. If you do, it's all too easy to find an excuse to drink if you have an argument with someone or someone says the "wrong thing". If you are doing it for yourself, you have no one to drive you to drink but yourself. No excuses!"

Today I learned...

Today I smiled because...

I have completed day...

9

Tomorrow I will...

DAY 10

Today I am grateful for...

Today I...

Will...

Won't...

I will treat myself to...

Date: _ _ _ _ _ _ _ _ _

Tip for the day

Read, read, read! There's never been more 'Quit Lit' than there is now. Reading other people's stories of how they stopped drinking and how their lives have improved is both inspirational and also occupies your time. There are also some great podcasts to listen to and videos to watch.

Visit the *Alcohol-Free Community* for articles and tips.

Today I learned...

Today I smiled because...

I have completed day...

10

Tomorrow I will...

DAY 11

Today I am grateful for...

Today I...

Will...

Won't...

I will treat myself to...

Date: __________

Tip for the day

If you need more face-to-face support, you may want to consider AA or a similar support group. They aren't for everyone but many people find them useful, especially in the early stages of recovery.

If you do go to a meeting (in person or online), don't be put off by the first one you go to if you don't like it. They are all different. Try at least a couple before making a final decision.

Today I learned...

Today I smiled because...

I have completed day...

11

Tomorrow I will...

Today I...

Will...

Won't...

I will treat myself to...

Date: __________

Tip for the day

"Don't be afraid to ask for help. Whether it's from friends and family, or a support group.

If you struggle alone, you are more likely to give in. Don't let the booze be your only friend. Many people have been where you are now and can, and will happily, give you help and advice."

Today I learned...

Today I smiled because...

I have completed day...

12

Tomorrow I will...

DAY 13

Today I am grateful for...

Today I...

Will...

Won't...

I will treat myself to...

Date: ___________

Tip for the day

"Join an online community such as the *Alcohol-Free Community* which has a private, free, and confidential group on Facebook. You can talk in confidence and without judgement. Whether your aim is to moderate your drinking, stop for good, or stay sober for a fixed period of time, you'll find lots of people who have done it before or are doing it now. They can support you. And as a bonus, you will be supporting them too!"

Today I learned...

Today I smiled because...

I have completed day...

13

Tomorrow I will...

DAY 14

Today I am grateful for...

Today I...

Will...

Won't...

I will treat myself to...

Date: _ _ _ _ _ _ _ _ _ _

Tip for the day

"Write a list of reasons you are stopping drinking. It's important to be brutally honest with yourself. Maybe take a photo of yourself to go with the list. If you can, put it somewhere visible such as your fridge door or your bedside table so you see it a lot during the coming weeks and months. There will be times when you try to trick yourself into forgetting why you are even doing this. Don't let your brain fool you, read your own words and remember your reasons!"

Today I learned...

Today I smiled because...

I have completed day...

14

Tomorrow I will...

Week 2 In Review

Date: __________

Things that have gone well...

Things that could have been better...

Things I learned about myself...

Next week I will...

Another week over, how are you feeling?

You're now half way through the first four weeks! How does that feel?

If you've managed to stay sober every day, give yourself a huge pat on the back! It's not easy and you're achieving something wonderful! But equally, if you've had the odd slip, don't beat yourself up. It happens to many people.

The most important thing is you keep trying and don't give up. As the Japanese proverb says – "Fall down seven times, stand up eight." Take each day as it comes and do your best to not pick up that first drink.

Work on improving your physical and mental fitness, as well as learning more about yourself – why you are here and where you want to be going forward.

By now you should have started to spot some triggers and examined why they happen and what you can do to cope with them. Sometimes it can be as simple as taking a different route home to avoid the off-licence or supermarket, but there will always be some triggers you can't avoid as easily. That's where you have to learn to cope with them and that's not always easy. It's time to grow up.

Many of us, especially those with drink problems, are often not as mature as our years would suggest. We've managed to avoid – or, at least tried to avoid – responsibilities that most people take for granted.

We've navigated the world of adulthood while often remaining, in many ways, child-like. Now is the time for that to change. It's never too late to mature and and it's vital we do if we are to stay on this path of self-improvement.

Remember Maslow's quote at the start of the book? "*In any given moment we have two options: to step forward into growth, or to step back into safety.*"

While stepping back into a life of drink may feel safe, it's actually the complete opposite.

ARE YOU READY TO STEP FORWARD? – <u>HERE'S WEEK THREE!</u>

DAY 15

Today I am grateful for...

Today I...

Will...

Won't...

I will treat myself to...

Date:

Tip for the day

"A lot of people drink when they're alone in the evenings. You may worry about long lonely nights ahead of you without the comfort of booze. If you sit there at 9pm and want to drink, just go to bed. This is a good time for the 'Quit-Lit' and to write your thoughts for the day here. Each morning, get up a little earlier. When you get up, do some exercise or chores. Your body clock will start to adjust to an earlier bed time, avoiding the 'wine-o-clock' alarm – and you'll sleep better too!"

Today I learned...

Today I smiled because...

I have completed day...

15

Tomorrow I will...

Today I...

Will...

Won't...

I will treat myself to...

Date: _ _ _ _ _ _ _ _ _

Tip for the day

“Accept that you may have a slip or two on your journey. In the same way better drivers often fail on their first driving test, sometimes it’s just part of the process. The important thing is to understand why you took a drink, and to get back to the plan as soon as possible. Sometimes people have one or two drinks, and stop immediately. Others may take a day or even longer, but the sooner you get back on track the better.”

Today I learned...

Today I smiled because...

I have completed day...

16

Tomorrow I will...

DAY 17

Today I am grateful for...

Today I...

Will...

Won't...

I will treat myself to...

Date: __________

Tip for the day

"If you do slip and take a drink when you didn't want to, don't be too hard on yourself. Giving up drink can be very tough.

Guilt, self-doubt and even self-hatred will make it even harder. You are only human, like all of us. No one is perfect and few people successfully beat it the first time they try."

Today I learned...

Today I smiled because...

I have completed day...

17

Tomorrow I will...

Today I...

Will...

Won't...

I will treat myself to...

Date: ________

Tip for the day

It's a popular saying that you have to reach rock bottom before you can start your recovery but your rock bottom doesn't have to be a near-death experience after losing your job, your house, and your friends and family! No one decides your rock bottom except you.

And no one who has become sober has ever said: "I wish I'd sunk lower and messed things up even more before I stopped drinking."

Today I learned...

Today I smiled because...

I have completed day...

18

Tomorrow I will...

DAY 19

Today I am grateful for...

Today I...

Will...

Won't...

I will treat myself to...

Date: __________

Tip for the day

Celebrate every win – no matter how small it may seem!

For instance, your first Friday night without a drink, the first time you go out for a meal without a drink, the first time you go to work without a hangover.

Whatever it may be, congratulate yourself – you deserve it!

Today I learned...

Today I smiled because...

I have completed day...

19

Tomorrow I will...

DAY 20

Today I am grateful for...

Today I...

Will...

Won't...

I will treat myself to...

Date: _ _ _ _ _ _ _ _ _

Tip for the day

Many people find it helps to reward themselves for milestones. You should be saving quite a bit of money by not drinking and, although you may be in debt and need to get your life back on track, it's important to reward yourself for your achievements.

Even if it's only small, a treat from yourself will give you something to look forward to and make you feel better!

Today I learned...

Today I smiled because...

I have completed day...

20

Tomorrow I will...

DAY 21

Today I am grateful for...

Today I...

Will...

Won't...

I will treat myself to...

Date: _ _ _ _ _ _ _ _ _

Tip for the day

Imagine your sober life. Think about the things you can do with a clear head and more time (and money!)

Compare that with how your life has been up until this point. Hopefully you'll realise which one is the better option.

Your future life is in your hands. Picture it, and then make it a reality!

Today I learned...

Today I smiled because...

I have completed day...

21

Tomorrow I will...

Week 3 In Review

Date: ____________

Things that have gone well...

Things that could have been better...

Things I learned about myself...

Next week I will...

You're almost there – just one last push to four weeks!

While the first week of giving up can be mentally draining and physically punishing, the challenges start to change as the weeks go by. Your initial enthusiasm may have worn off by now and, for many, this is when other problems can crop up. This is a great time to go back to the start of this journal and read how you felt in the first week.

It's not unusual for people to say they want to drink because they feel bored and isolated, and they think that drinking will help. But ask yourself honestly why drinking would stop you being bored and isolated. Why would a drink help?

If your friends don't want to be with you unless you are drinking, you probably need to find new friends. It may sound harsh, but you need people around you who are supportive, not people who want to sabotage your recovery.

What to do instead of drinking?

Find something to occupy yourself. It can be hard to adjust when drinking has been your main hobby. But there are so many other things that you can do instead that will stop you feeling like this. From tedious, but important, things like cleaning the house, decorating a room, making holiday or career plans, or simply going out for a walk in the park and taking in nature.

There are a million things you can do that don't involve having a drink, and before you know it the day is over and – hopefully – you've had a great time! At the very least you've managed another day without a drink – and you might have a clean house too! Each day you do that takes you one step closer to your goal of a better life and a better you.

In Marathon running, most people say the hardest miles are 18 to 23. That equates to the next few days. But as you see the finishing line for the first four weeks in sight, the last few days of the week will get easier and easier!

KEEP GOING – <u>YOU'VE ALMOST DONE IT!</u>

DAY 22

Today I am grateful for...

Today I...

Will...

Won't...

I will treat myself to...

Date: __________

Tip for the day

"Being sober doesn't mean life will always be perfect. Bad things happen to everyone no matter what. We can all lose loved ones – pets, friends, family – we may lose jobs, and we may become ill.

It's at times like this you may want to turn to drink to cope but it's much easier to deal with problems when you are sober than it is with a cloudy mind."

Today I learned...

Today I smiled because...

I have completed day...

22

Tomorrow I will...

DAY 23

Today I am grateful for...

Today I...

Will...

Won't...

I will treat myself to...

Date: __________

Tip for the day

"You'll probably find you have a lot of free time on your hands. For many of us, drinking becomes "what we do". When we stop, there's a void that needs filling. In fact, one of the reasons some people find it hard to stop is precisely because they're worried they will have nothing worth living for. This couldn't be farther from the truth. Drink sucks up time you can use for much better things. Write a list of things you haven't done yet and start doing them now!"

Today I learned...

Today I smiled because...

I have completed day...

23

Tomorrow I will...

DAY 24

Today I am grateful for...

Today I...

Will...

Won't...

I will treat myself to...

Date: __________

Tip for the day

> Many drinkers don't have a great diet. Taking up cooking is not only a good way to eat more healthily, but you're likely to save money too. It also keeps you busy and can distract you during the early evening. Just keep a wary eye out for recipes that include alcohol (no, it doesn't burn off!) There are lots of ways to substitute alcohol in recipes – such as alcohol-free wine or even tea – but there are many great recipes that don't need alcohol in the first place!

Today I learned...

Today I smiled because...

I have completed day...

24

Tomorrow I will...

DAY 25

Today I am grateful for...

Today I...

Will...

Won't...

I will treat myself to...

Date: __________

Tip for the day

"While there are dozens of reasons you can give for saying no if someone is hassling you to have a drink, the best one is three simple words. "I don't drink." You don't need to explain yourself to anyone and you shouldn't be ashamed of what you do with your body.

"I don't drink." not only makes it clear to them, but it also re-enforces the fact to yourself. And sometimes we all need that reminder."

Today I learned...

Today I smiled because...

I have completed day...

25

Tomorrow I will...

DAY 26

Today I am grateful for...

Today I...

Will...

Won't...

I will treat myself to...

Date: _ _ _ _ _ _ _ _ _

Tip for the day

Pamper yourself. If you find yourself at a loss for something to do in the evening and you're feeling stressed, take a relaxing bath with some natural bath oils and candles. Tell your family you want some time for yourself. Even something as simple as colouring your roots or giving yourself a pedicure can make you feel better.

If you can afford it, book a spa day for a special treat.

Today I learned...

Today I smiled because...

I have completed day...

26

Tomorrow I will...

DAY 27

Today I am grateful for...

Today I...

Will...

Won't...

I will treat myself to...

Date: _ _ _ _ _ _ _ _ _

Tip for the day

"While real friends will understand why you are stopping drinking and want to support you, that isn't always the case. Many people you consider friends are really only drinking friends.

They can feel threatened and become defensive when you quit because it highlights their own drinking problem. No one wants to lose friends, but your health and your life matters more right now."

Today I learned...

Today I smiled because...

I have completed day...

27

Tomorrow I will...

DAY 28!

Today I am grateful for...

Today I...

Will...

Won't...

I will treat myself to...

Date: ___________

Tip for the day

"If you've managed to get through these first four weeks without a drink, congratulations! Your body is now long clear of alcohol. As physical cravings are a thing of the past, if you still feel rough, it's either another reason (in which case do speak to your doctor), or it's psychological. The psychological battle is very real and can continue for a long time.
For some people it's a lifelong battle, but it does get easier over time."

Today I learned...

Today I smiled because...

I have completed day...

28

Tomorrow I will...

Week 4 In Review

Date: __________

Things that have gone well...

Things that could have been better...

Things I learned about myself...

Next week I will...

And... breathe!

Well done, the first four weeks are now over! But there are no winners or losers here. There's only one person in this contest and that's you.

The fact you've got this far is a victory in itself. If you've managed to stay sober – that's fantastic, truly fantastic, and you should be very proud of yourself. You've done something that you possibly thought was impossible four weeks ago.

If you've had some ups and downs but you're still here, that's also fantastic and you should still be very proud of yourself for not giving up on giving up!

This is a journey that many have done before, and one you can do with other people. But ultimately it is one you do alone. It's not a race. It's not a competition. You don't need to "win" against anyone, you just need to beat the booze.

So, what next?

Spend some time reviewing your journal. Remind yourself how you felt when you first started, and the hardships – and pleasures – you've experienced over the last four weeks. Evaluate the month.

Make sure you are clear about your triggers, your goals, your hopes, your desires, and prepare yourself for the next stage. Giving up is an incredible achievement, but the real challenge is to stay sober going forward.

The next section of this journal covers week 5 to week 12. These are likely to be a different kind of hard. All your physical addictions are long gone and now the fight is purely with your own mind.

Keep going, and smash those 12 *weeks To A Sober Life*!

Most of all, remember:

YOU ARE DOING THIS FOR <u>YOU</u> – AND <u>YOU ARE AMAZING!</u>

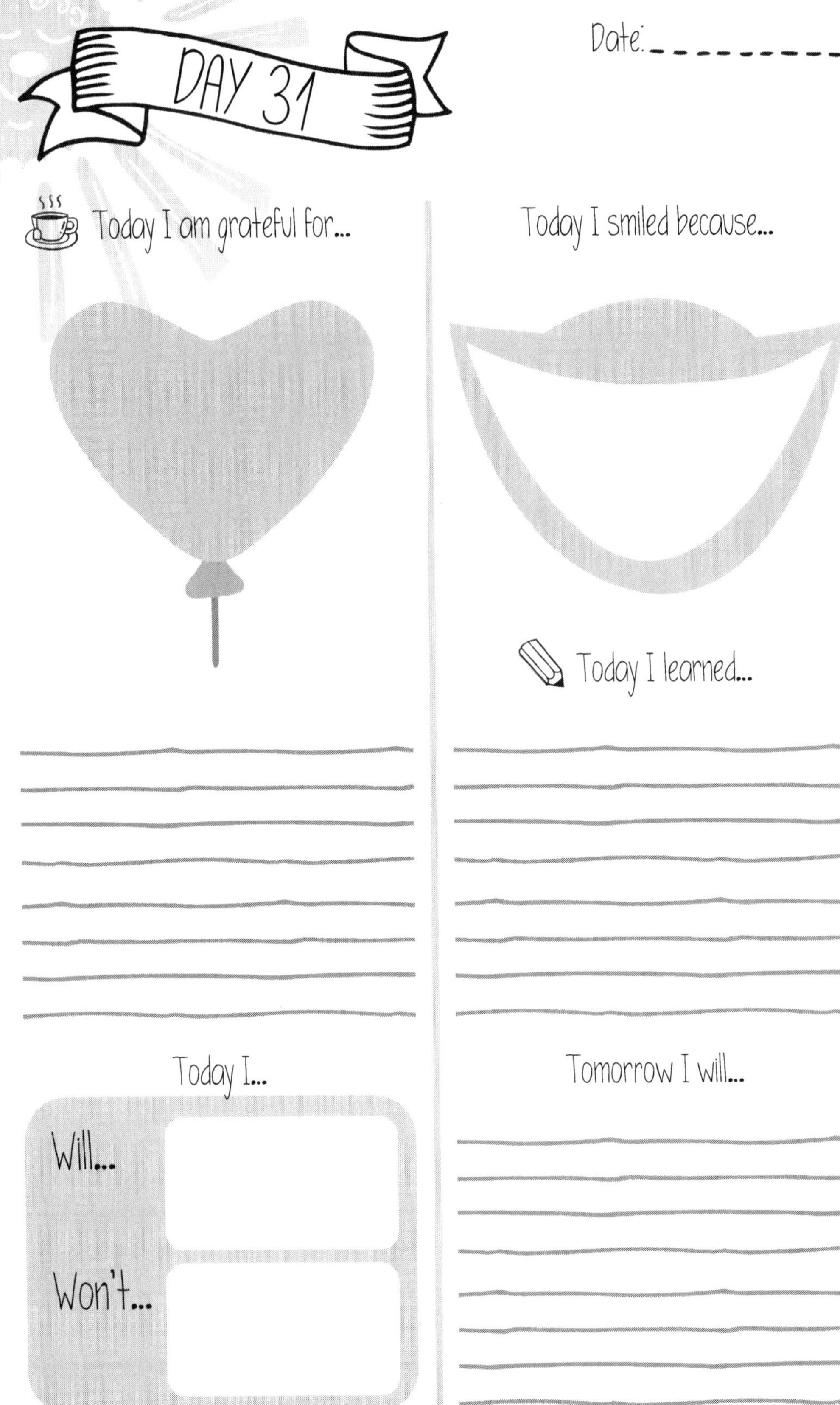
DAY 31
Date:
Today I am grateful for...
Today I smiled because...
Today I learned...
Today I...
Will...
Won't...
Tomorrow I will...

Date: ____________

Today I am grateful for...

Today I smiled because...

Today I learned...

Today I...

Will...

Won't...

Tomorrow I will...

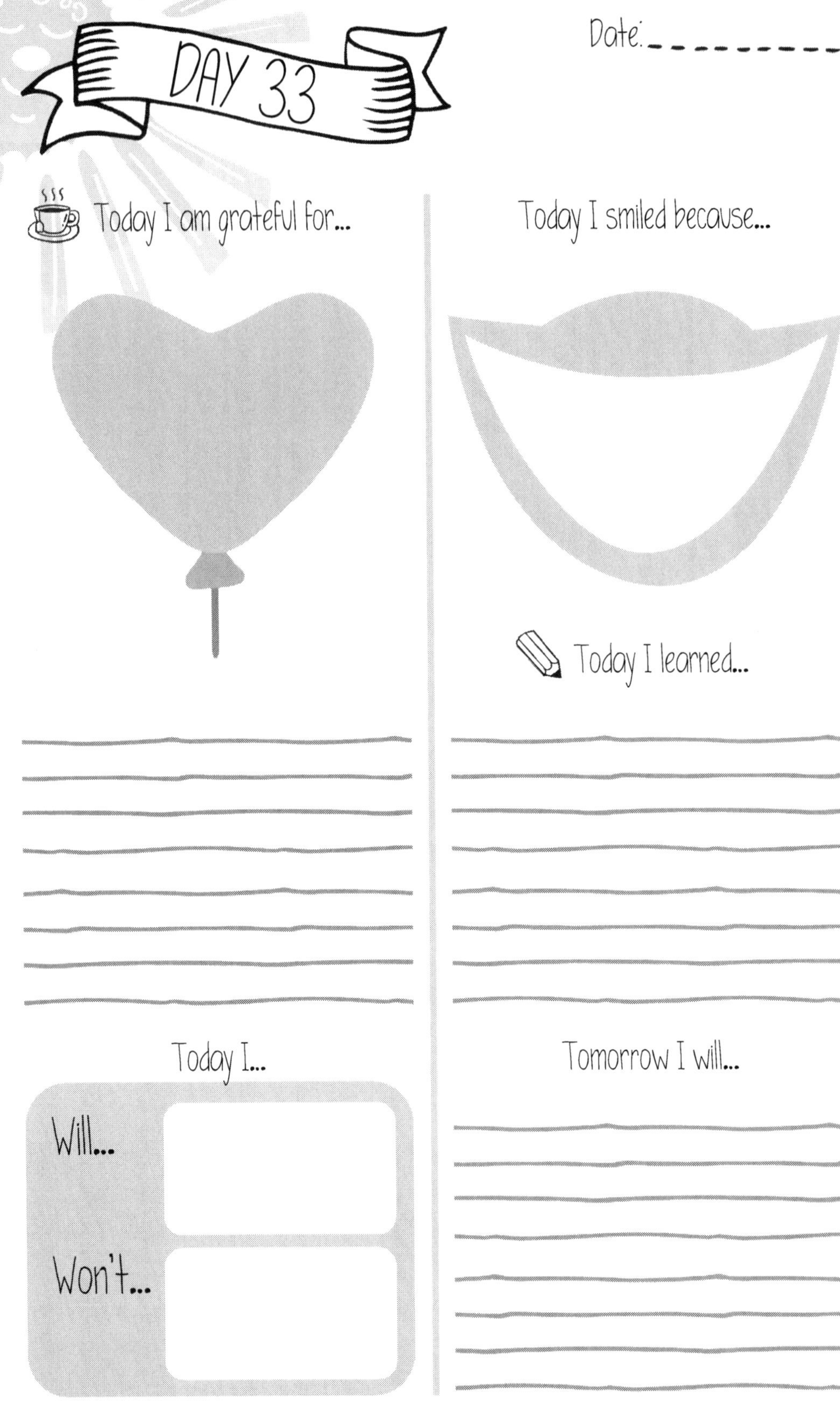
DAY 33
Date:
Today I am grateful for...
Today I smiled because...
Today I learned...
Today I...
Will...
Won't...
Tomorrow I will...

Date: ....

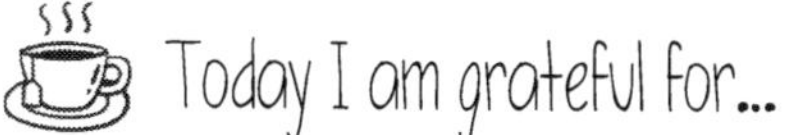

Today I learned...

Today I...

Tomorrow I will...

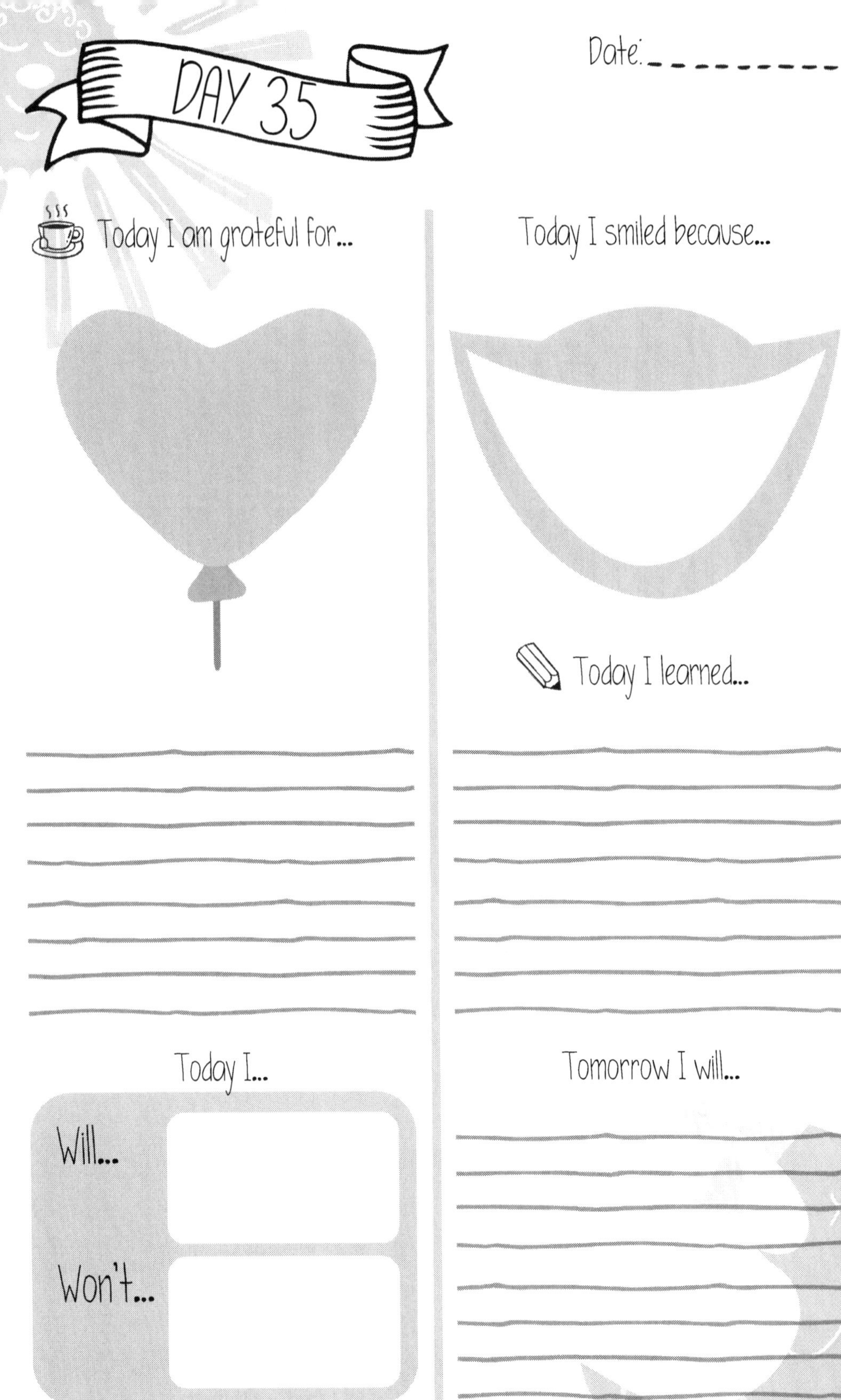

DAY 35
Date:
Today I am grateful for...
Today I smiled because...
Today I learned...
Today I...
Will...
Won't...
Tomorrow I will...

Week 5 In Review

Date: __________

Things that have gone well...

Things that could have been better...

Things I learned about myself...

Next week I will...

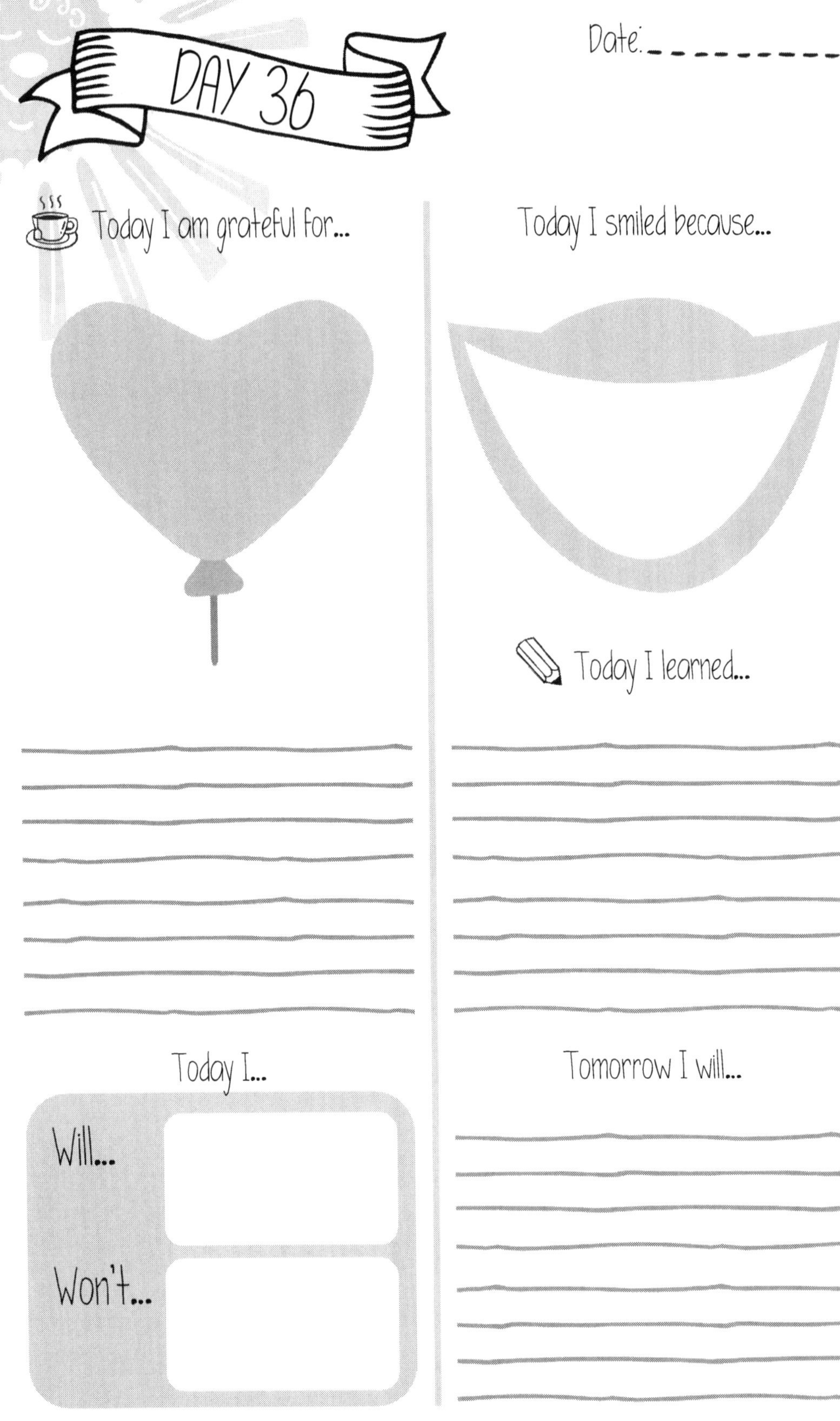
DAY 36
Date:
Today I am grateful for...
Today I smiled because...
Today I learned...
Today I...
Will...
Won't...
Tomorrow I will...

Date:

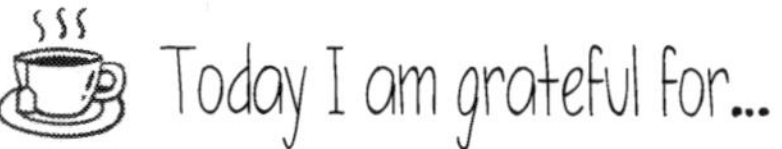

Today I smiled because...

Today I learned...

Today I...

Will...

Won't...

Tomorrow I will...

DAY 38
Date:
Today I am grateful for...
Today I smiled because...
Today I learned...
Today I...
Will...
Won't...
Tomorrow I will...

Date: ___________

Today I am grateful for...

Today I smiled because...

Today I learned...

Today I...

Will...

Won't...

Tomorrow I will...

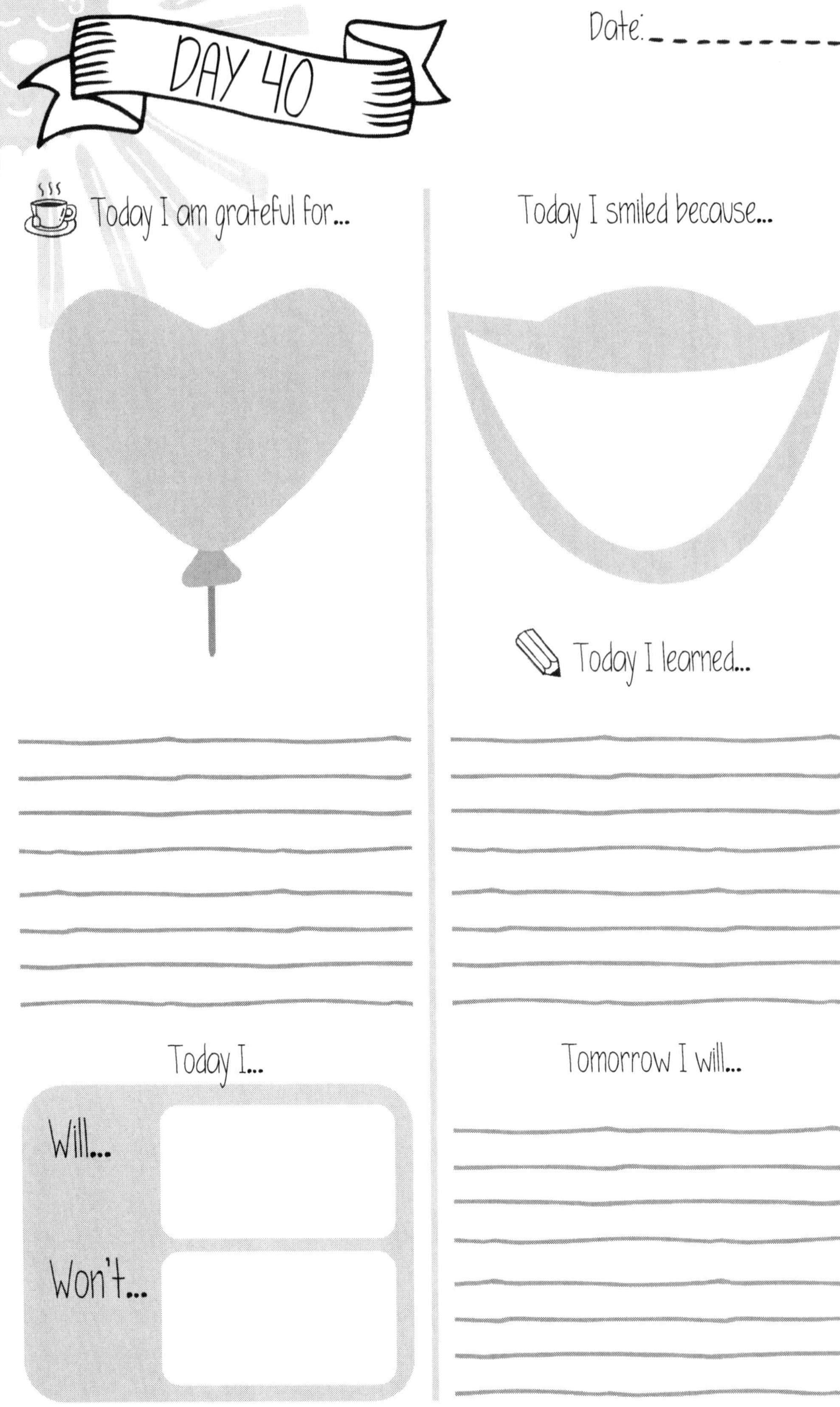
DAY 40
Date:
Today I am grateful for...
Today I smiled because...
Today I learned...
Today I...
Will...
Won't...
Tomorrow I will...

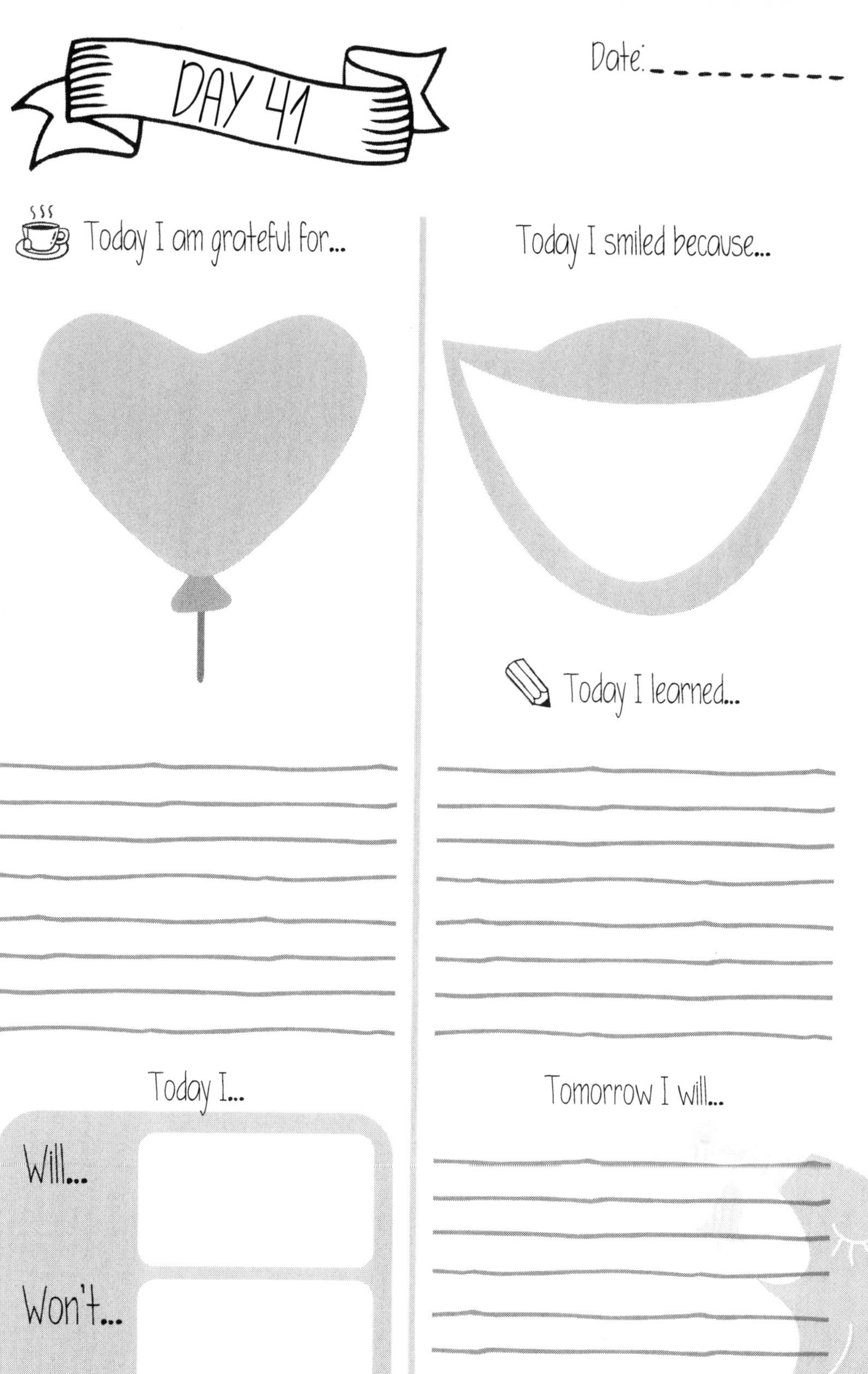
DAY 41
Date:
Today I am grateful for...
Today I smiled because...
Today I learned...
Today I...
Will...
Won't...
Tomorrow I will...

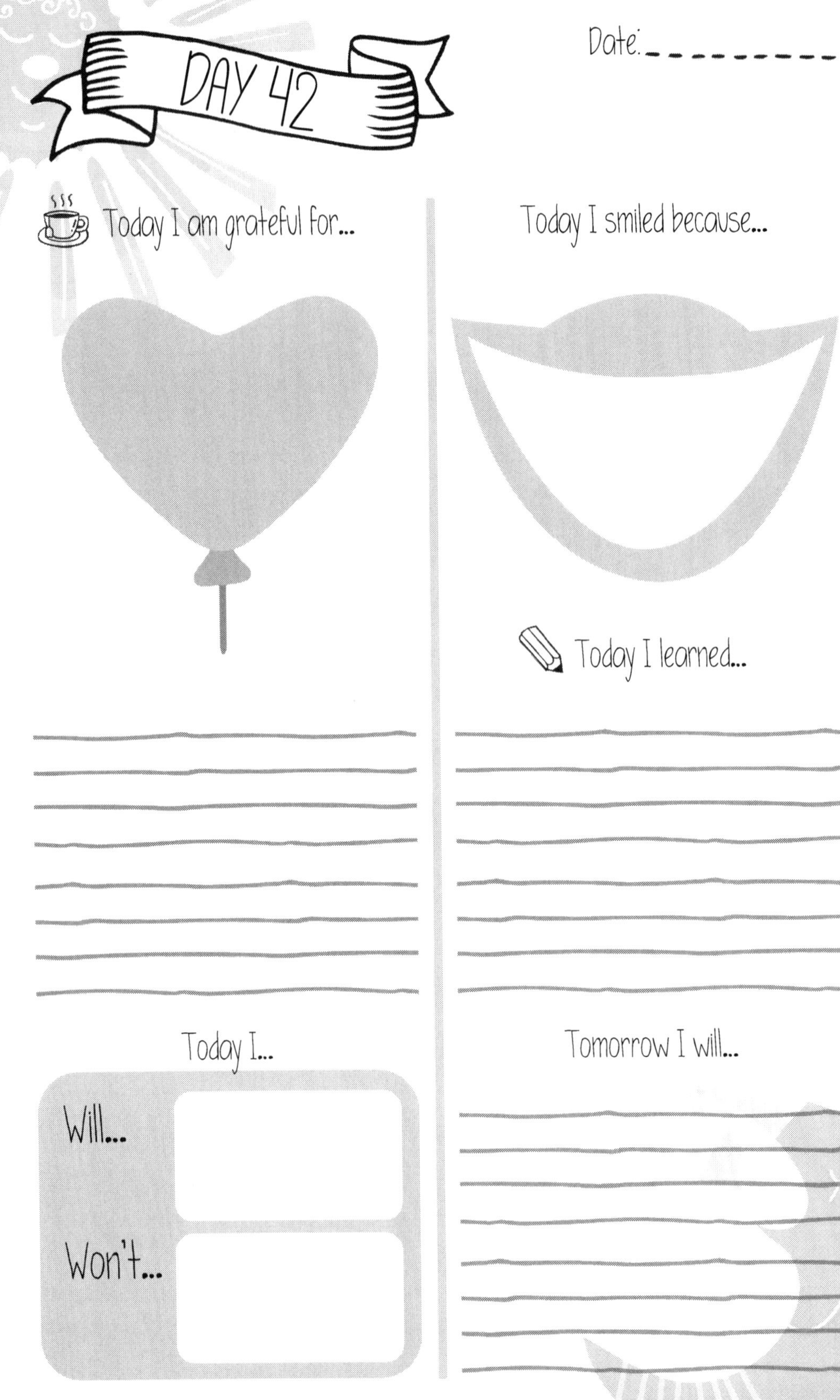
DAY 42
Date:
Today I am grateful for...
Today I smiled because...
Today I learned...
Today I...
Will...
Won't...
Tomorrow I will...

Week 6 In Review

Date: ________

Things that have gone well...

Things that could have been better...

Things I learned about myself...

Next week I will...

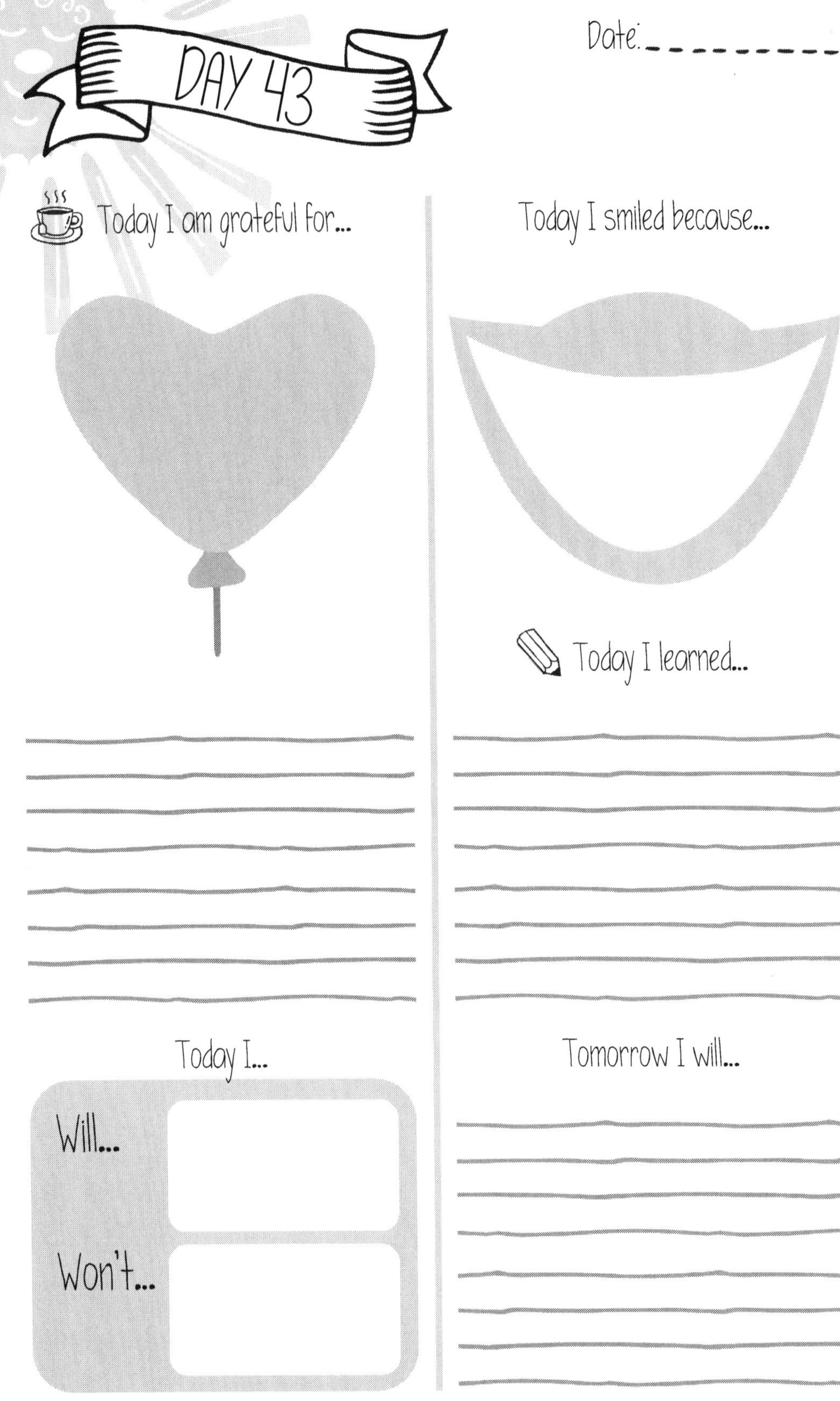
DAY 43
Date:
Today I am grateful for...
Today I smiled because...
Today I learned...
Today I...
Will...
Won't...
Tomorrow I will...

Date: _________

Today I...

Will...

Won't...

Tomorrow I will...

Date: ________

Today I am grateful for...

Today I smiled because...

Today I learned...

Today I...

Will...

Won't...

Tomorrow I will...

Date: __________

Today I am grateful for...

Today I smiled because...

Today I learned...

Today I...

Will...

Won't...

Tomorrow I will...

DAY 47
Date:
Today I am grateful for...
Today I smiled because...
Today I learned...
Today I...
Will...
Won't...
Tomorrow I will...

Date: __________

Today I am grateful for...

Today I smiled because...

Today I learned...

Today I...

Will...

Won't...

Tomorrow I will...

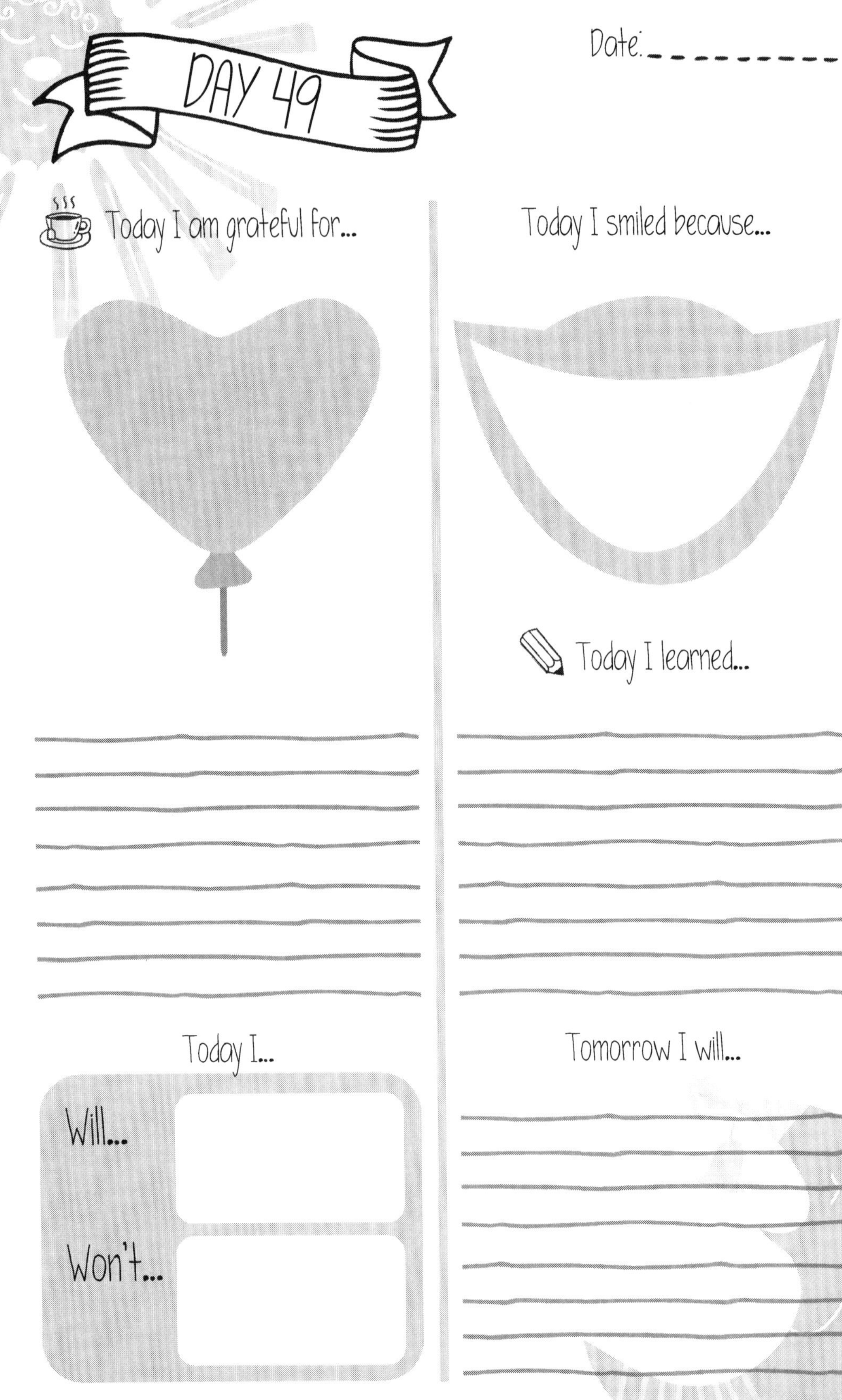

DAY 49

Date: _________

Today I am grateful for...

Today I smiled because...

Today I learned...

Today I...

Will...

Won't...

Tomorrow I will...

Week 7 In Review

Date: ___________

Things that have gone well...

Things that could have been better...

Things I learned about myself...

Next week I will...

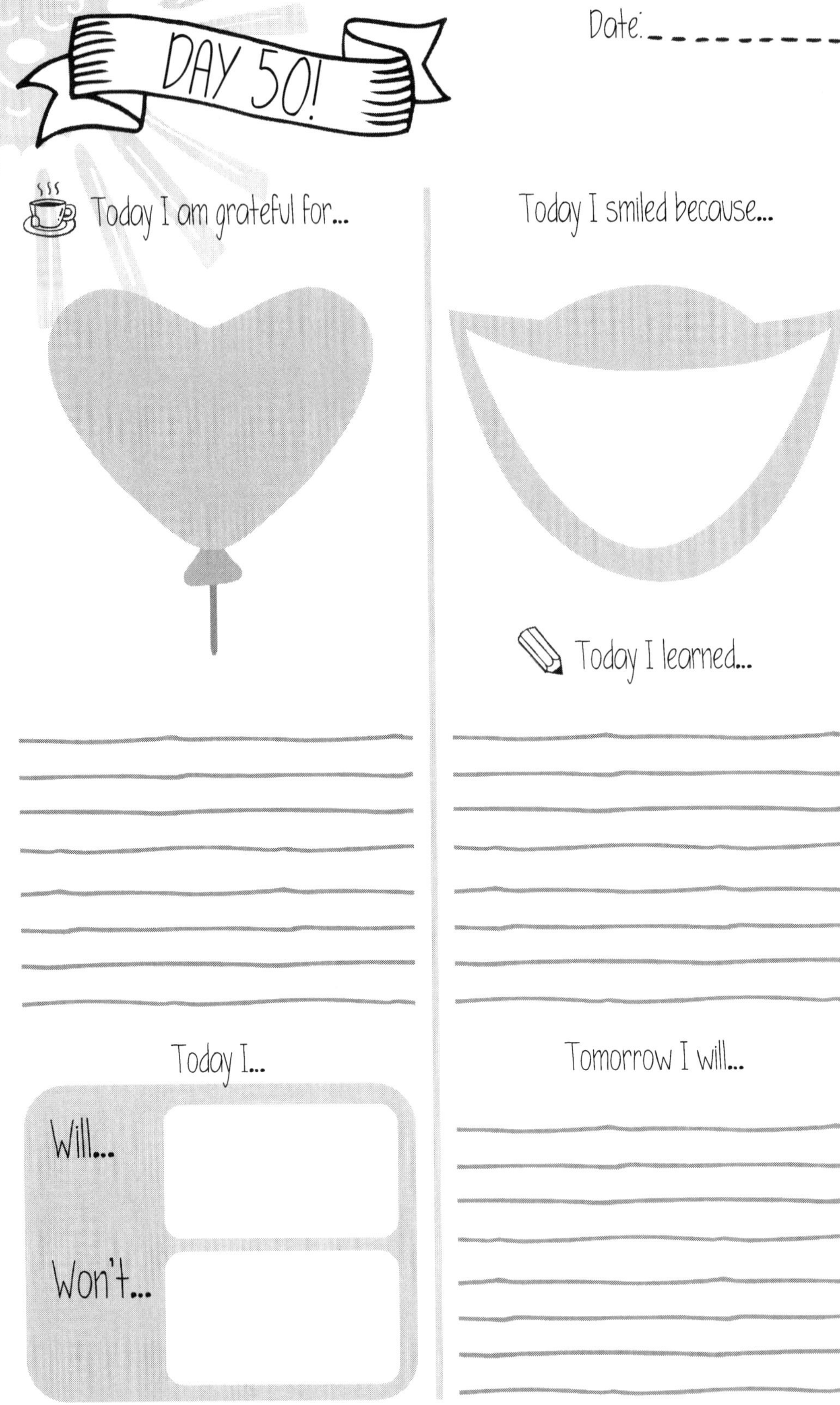
DAY 50!
Date:
Today I am grateful for...
Today I smiled because...
Today I learned...
Today I...
Will...
Won't...
Tomorrow I will...

Date: ___________

Today I am grateful for...

Today I smiled because...

Today I learned...

Today I...

Will...

Won't...

Tomorrow I will...

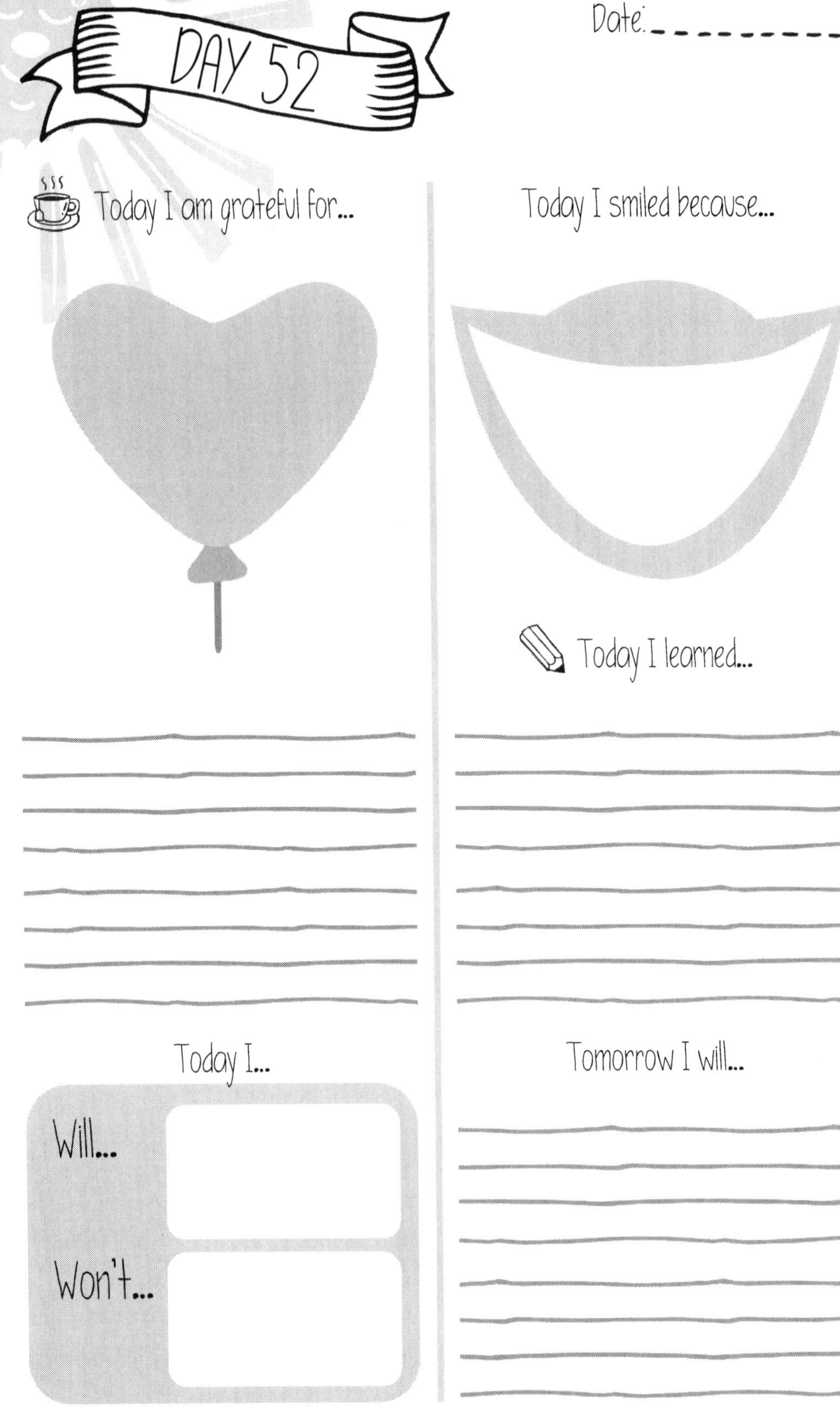
DAY 52
Date:
Today I am grateful for...
Today I smiled because...
Today I learned...
Today I...
Will...
Won't...
Tomorrow I will...

DAY 53

Date: __________

Today I am grateful for...

Today I smiled because...

Today I learned...

Today I...

Will...

Won't...

Tomorrow I will...

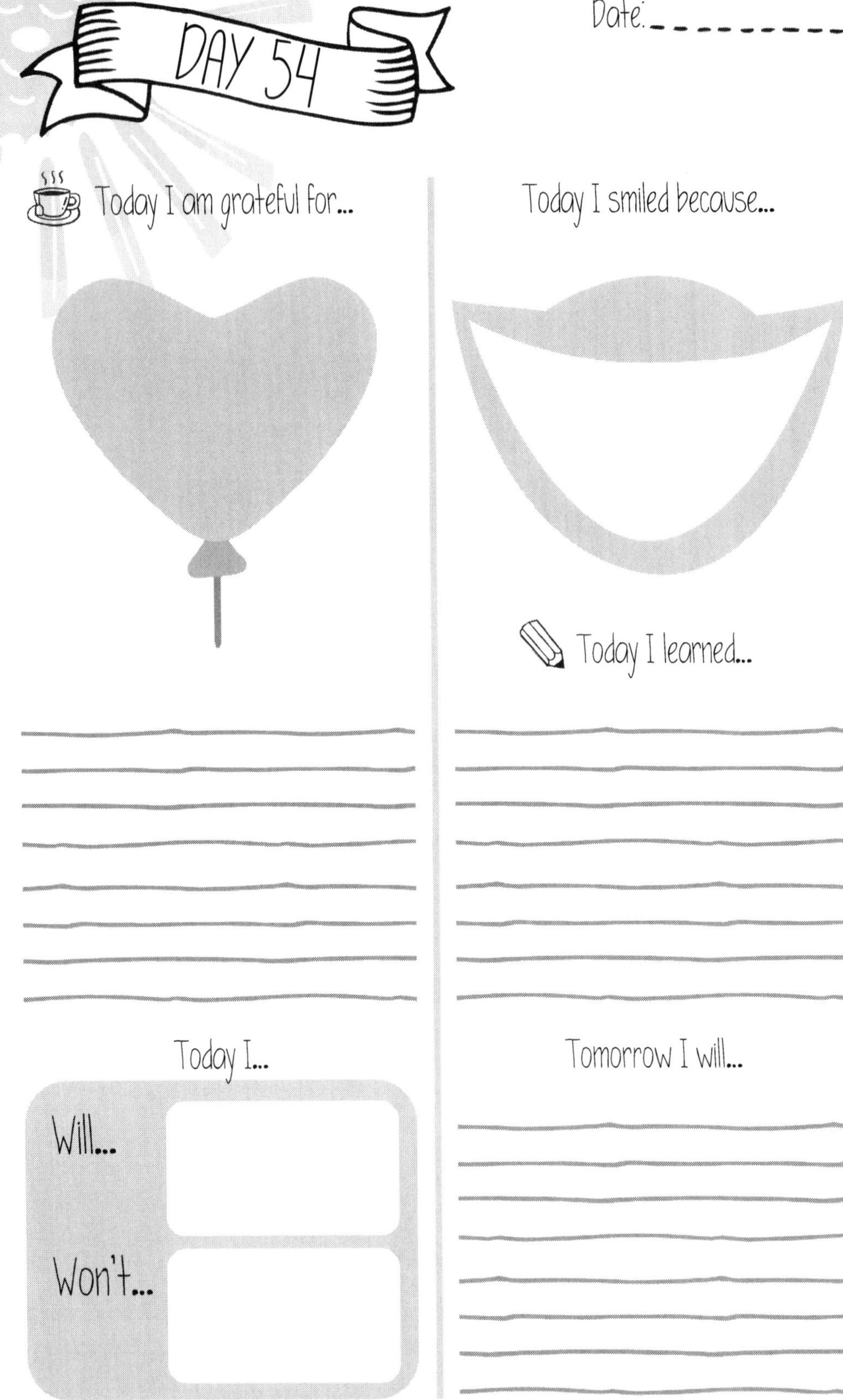
DAY 54
Date:
Today I am grateful for...
Today I smiled because...
Today I learned...
Today I...
Will...
Won't...
Tomorrow I will...

Date: ____________

Today I am grateful for...

Today I smiled because...

Today I learned...

Today I...

Will...

Won't...

Tomorrow I will...

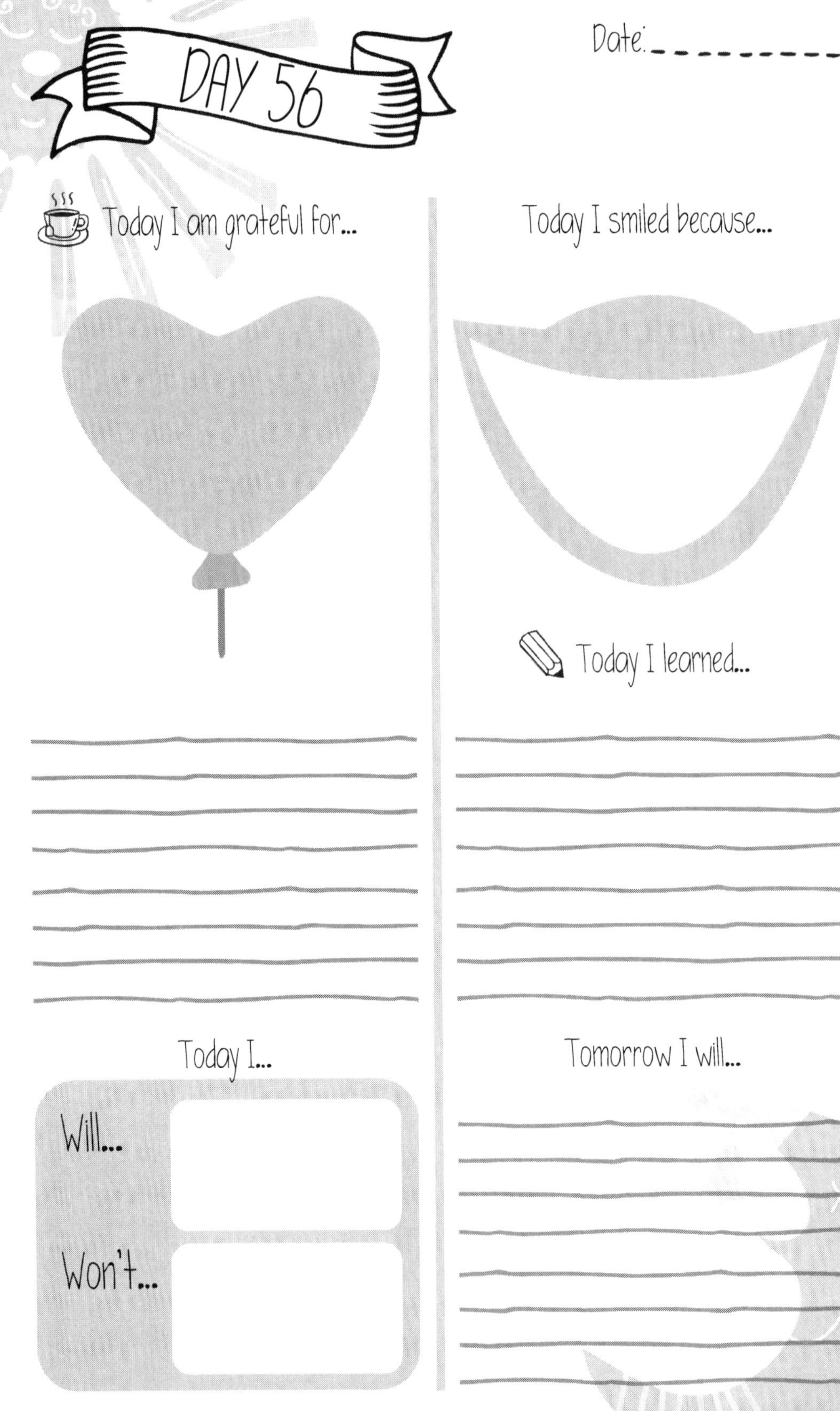
DAY 56
Date:
Today I am grateful for...
Today I smiled because...
Today I learned...
Today I...
Will...
Won't...
Tomorrow I will...

Week 8 In Review

Date: ___________

Things that have gone well...

Things that could have been better...

Things I learned about myself...

Next week I will...

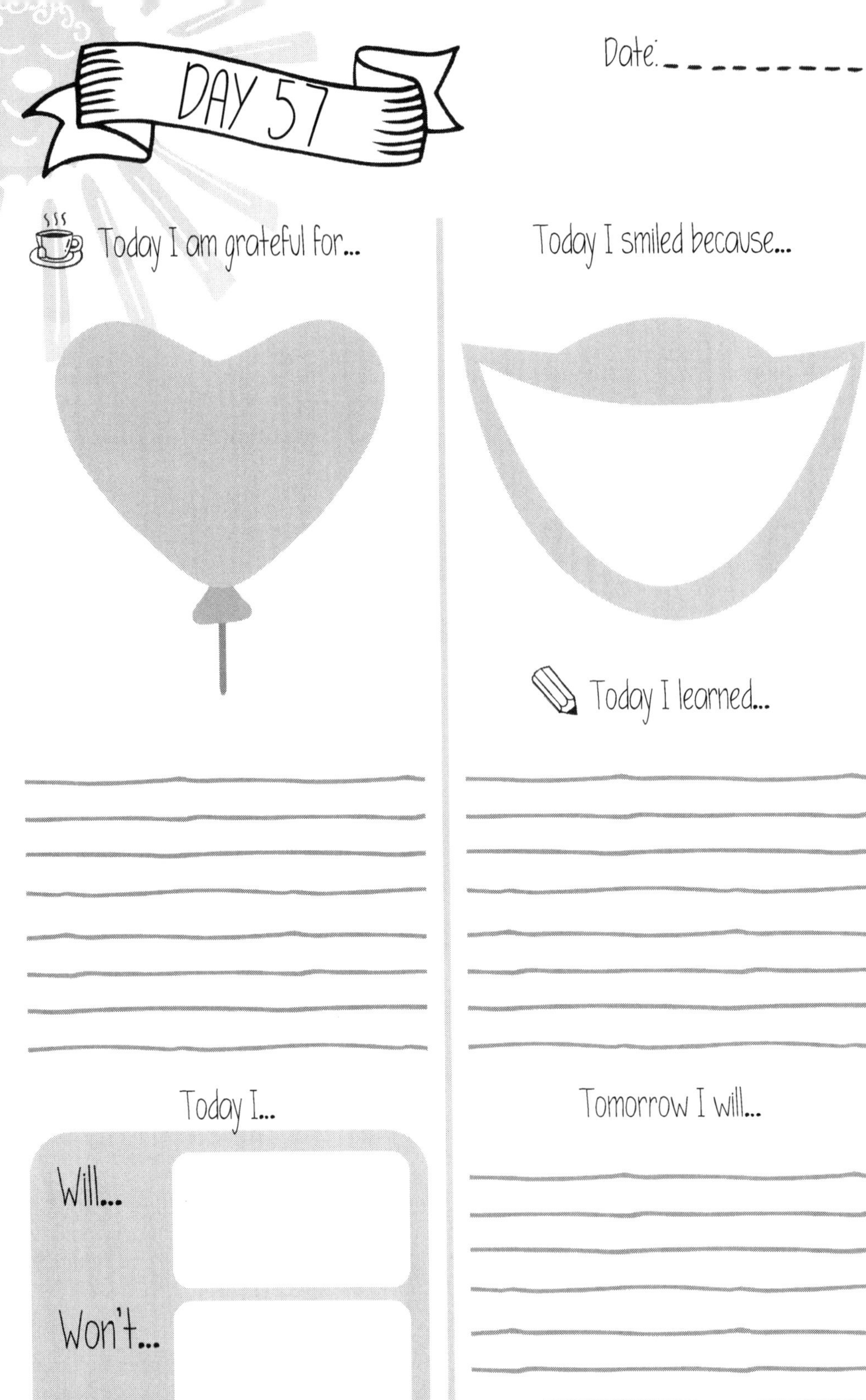

DAY 57
Date:
Today I am grateful for...
Today I smiled because...
Today I learned...
Today I...
Will...
Won't...
Tomorrow I will...

Date:__________

Today I am grateful for...

Today I smiled because...

Today I learned...

Today I...

Will...

Won't...

Tomorrow I will...

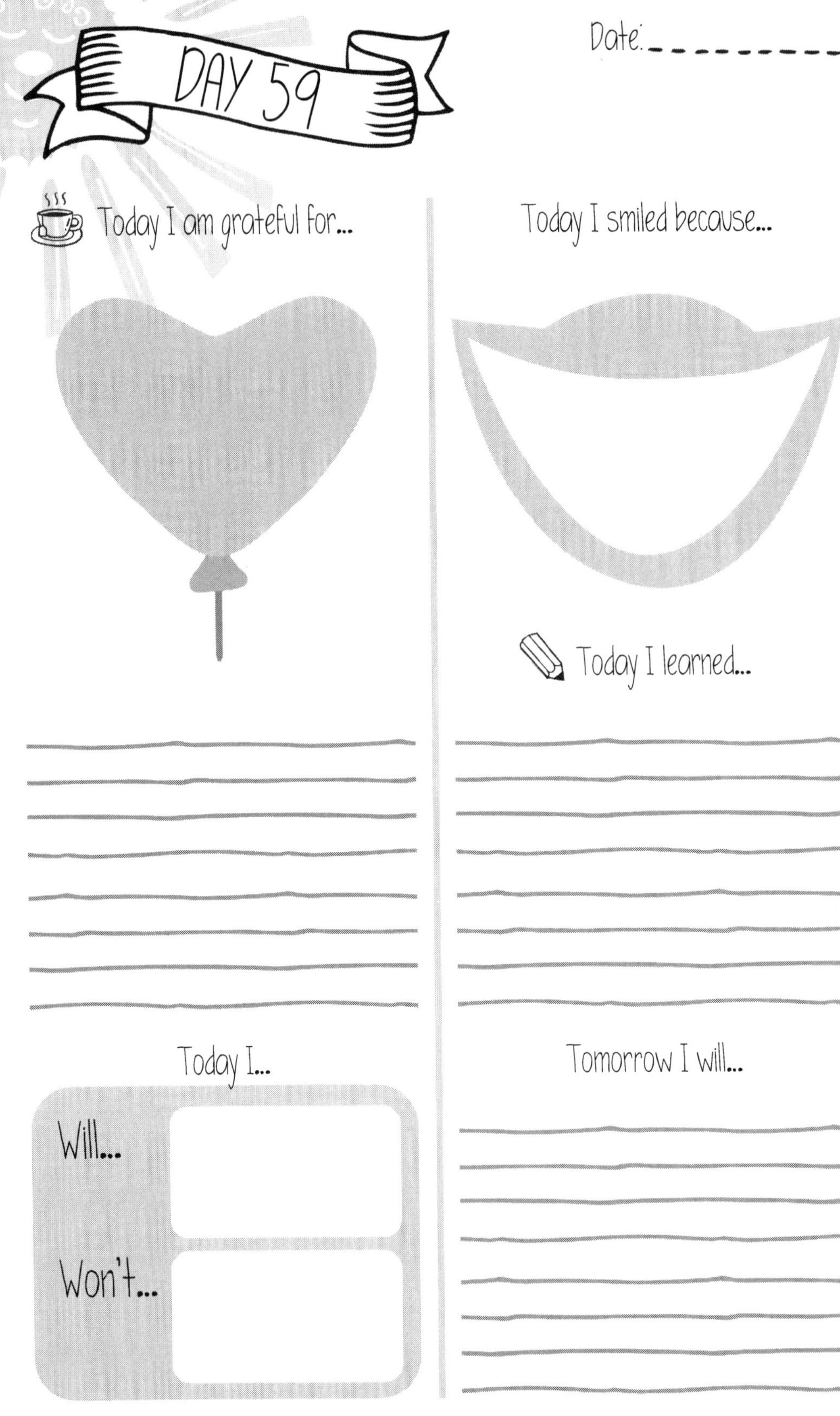

DAY 59

Date:

Today I am grateful for...

Today I smiled because...

Today I learned...

Today I...

Will...

Won't...

Tomorrow I will...

Date: __________

Today I am grateful for...

Today I smiled because...

Today I learned...

Today I...

Will...

Won't...

Tomorrow I will...

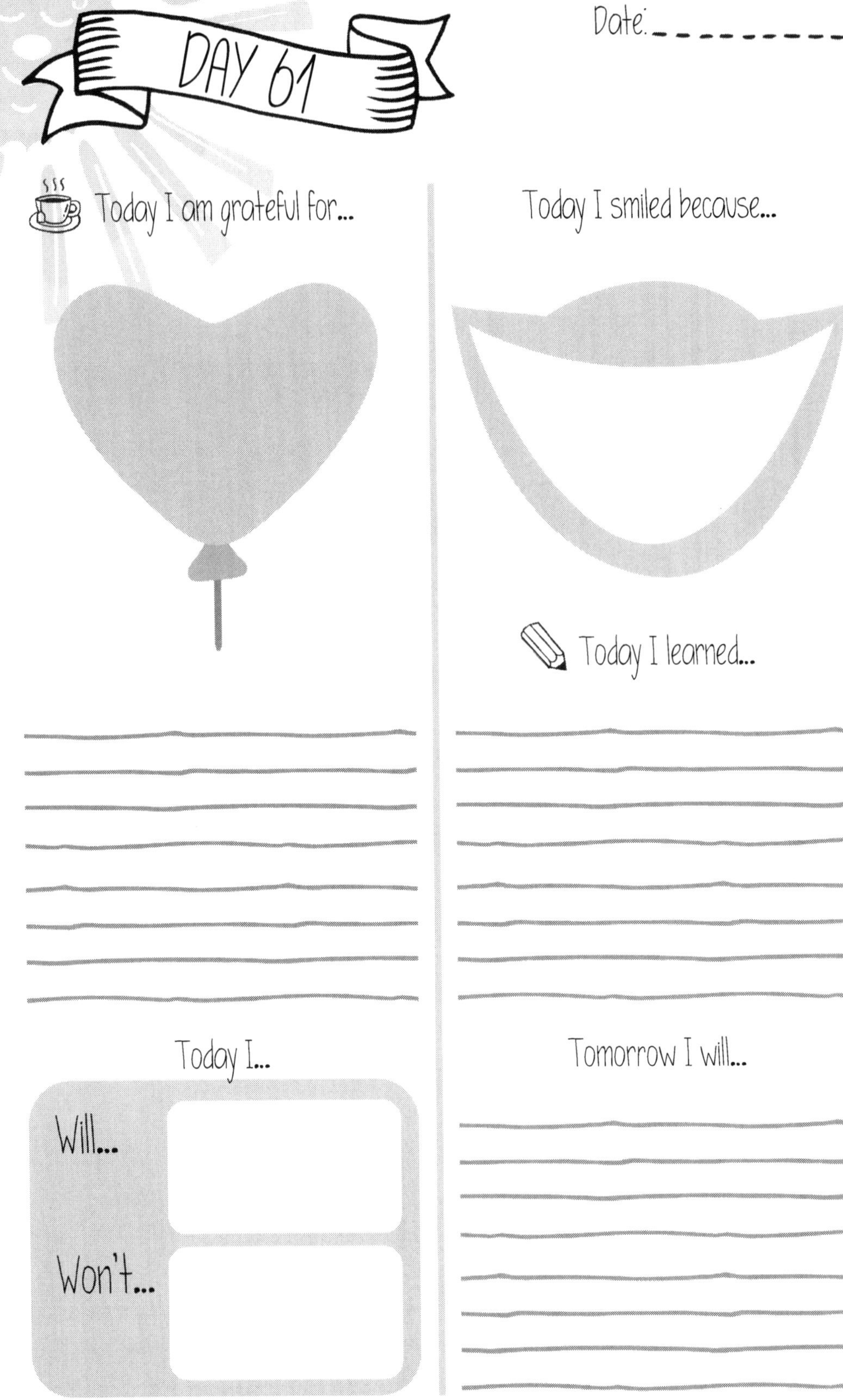
DAY 61
Date:
Today I am grateful for...
Today I smiled because...
Today I learned...
Today I...
Will...
Won't...
Tomorrow I will...

Date: __________

Today I am grateful for...

Today I smiled because...

Today I learned...

Today I...

Will...

Won't...

Tomorrow I will...

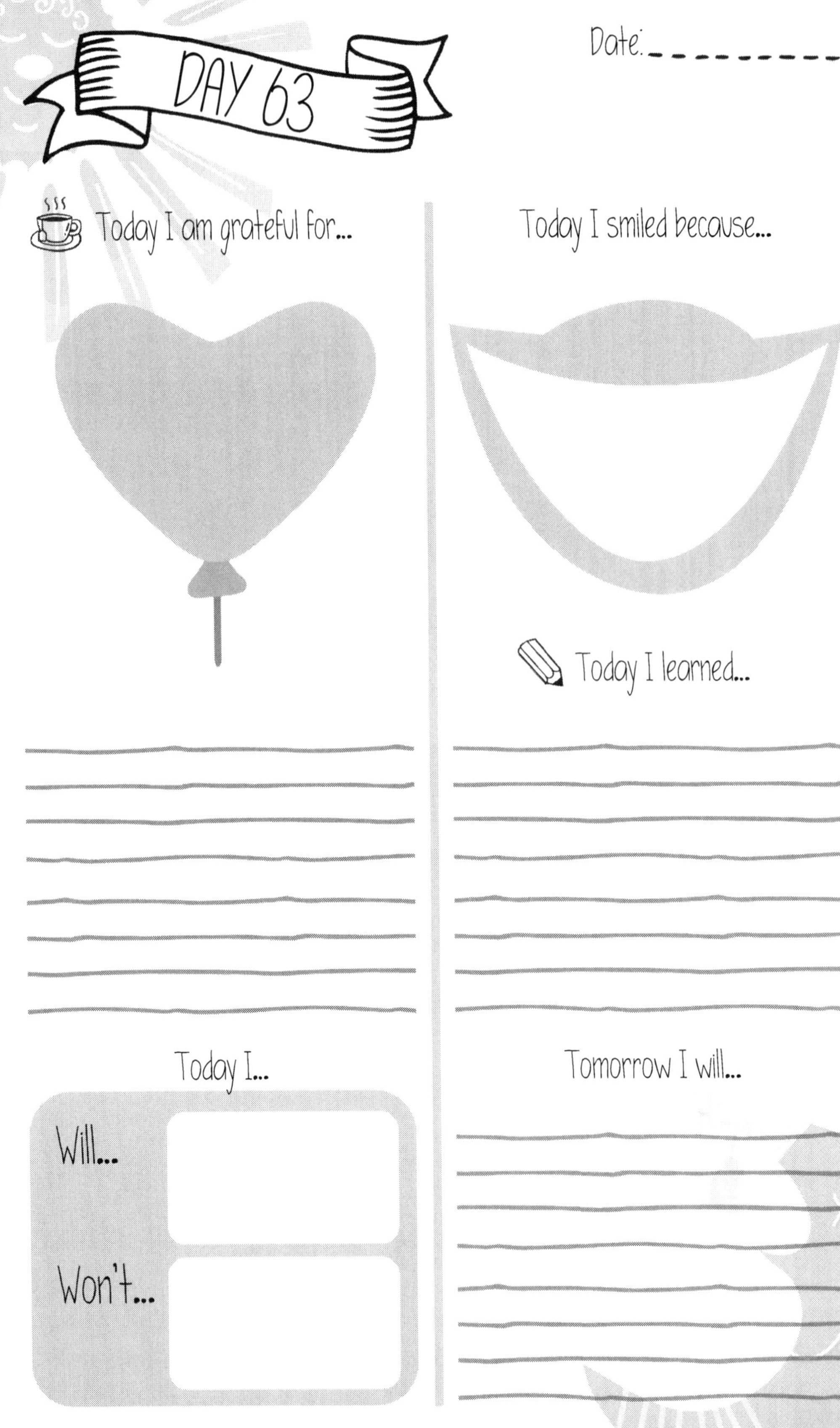

DAY 63

Date:_________

Today I am grateful for...

Today I smiled because...

Today I learned...

Today I...

Will...

Won't...

Tomorrow I will...

Week 9 In Review

Date: __________

Things that have gone well...

Things that could have been better...

Things I learned about myself...

Next week I will...

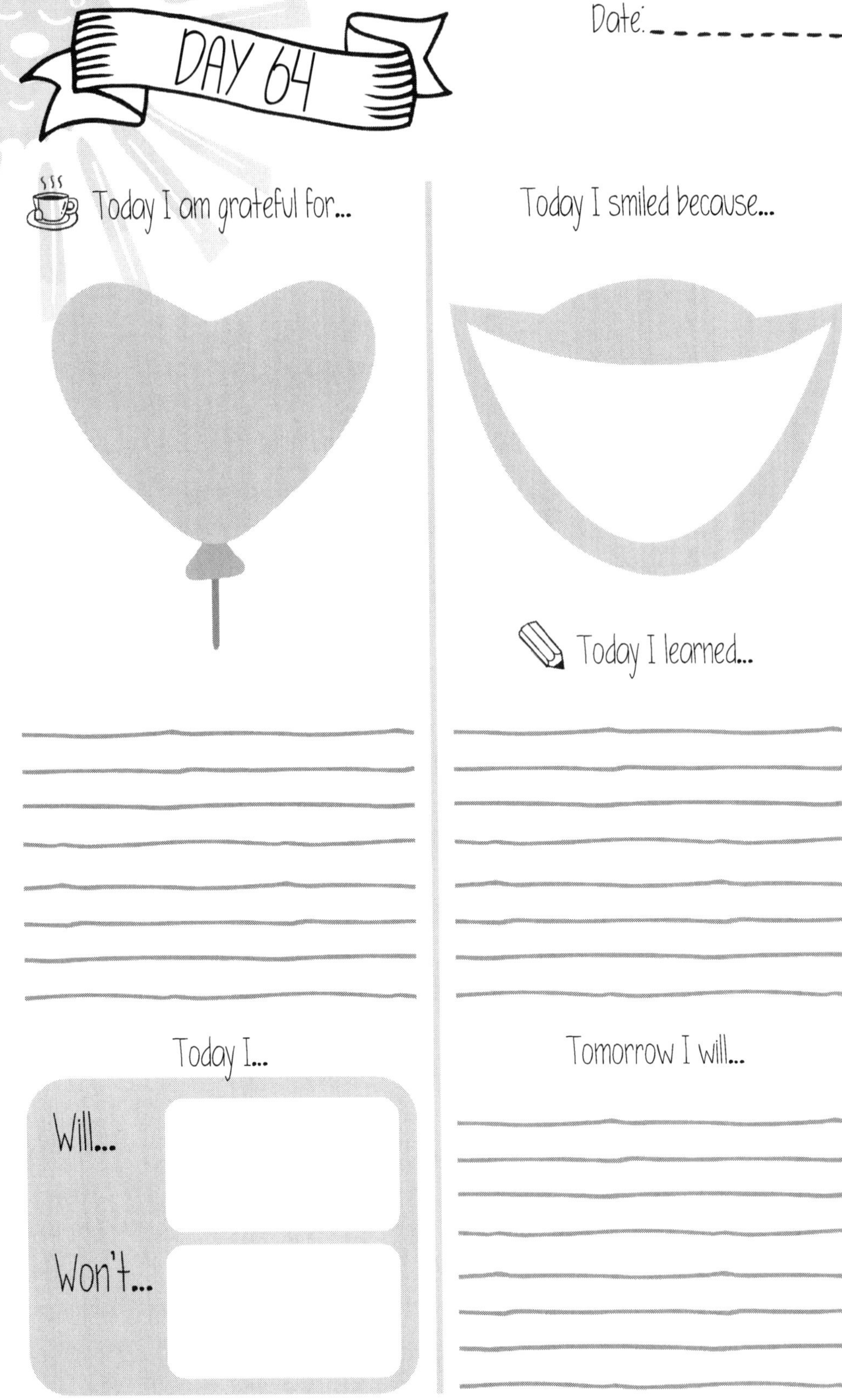
DAY 64
Date:
Today I am grateful for...
Today I smiled because...
Today I learned...
Today I...
Will...
Won't...
Tomorrow I will...

Date:

Today I am grateful for...

Today I smiled because...

Today I learned...

Today I...

Will...

Won't...

Tomorrow I will...

DAY 66

Date:__________

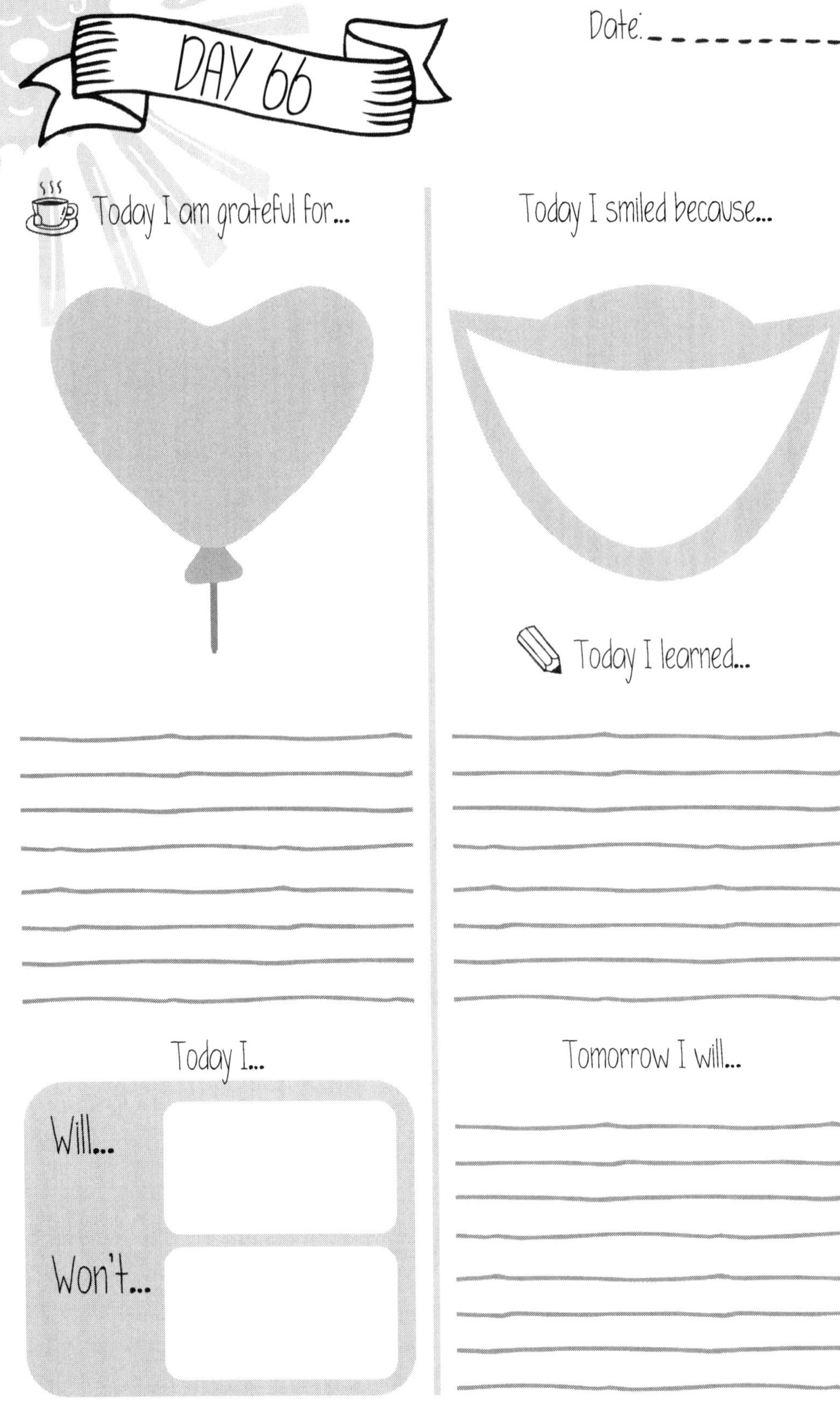

Today I am grateful for...

Today I smiled because...

Today I learned...

Today I...

Will...

Won't...

Tomorrow I will...

DAY 67
Date:
Today I am grateful for...
Today I smiled because...
Today I learned...
Today I...
Will...
Won't...
Tomorrow I will...

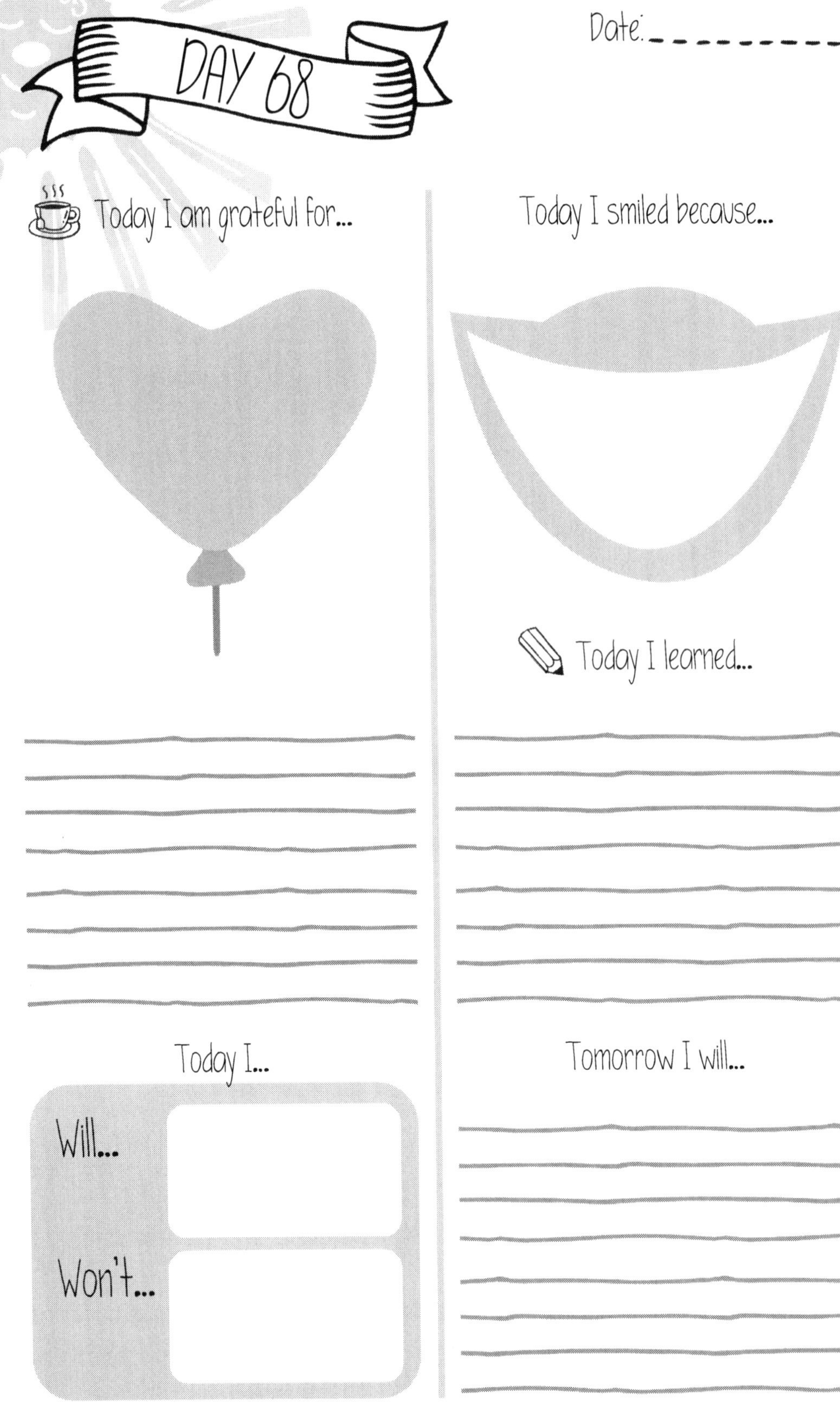

DAY 68

Date: ________

Today I am grateful for...

Today I smiled because...

Today I learned...

Today I...

Will...

Won't...

Tomorrow I will...

Date: ___________

Today I am grateful for...

Today I smiled because...

Today I learned...

Today I...

Will...

Won't...

Tomorrow I will...

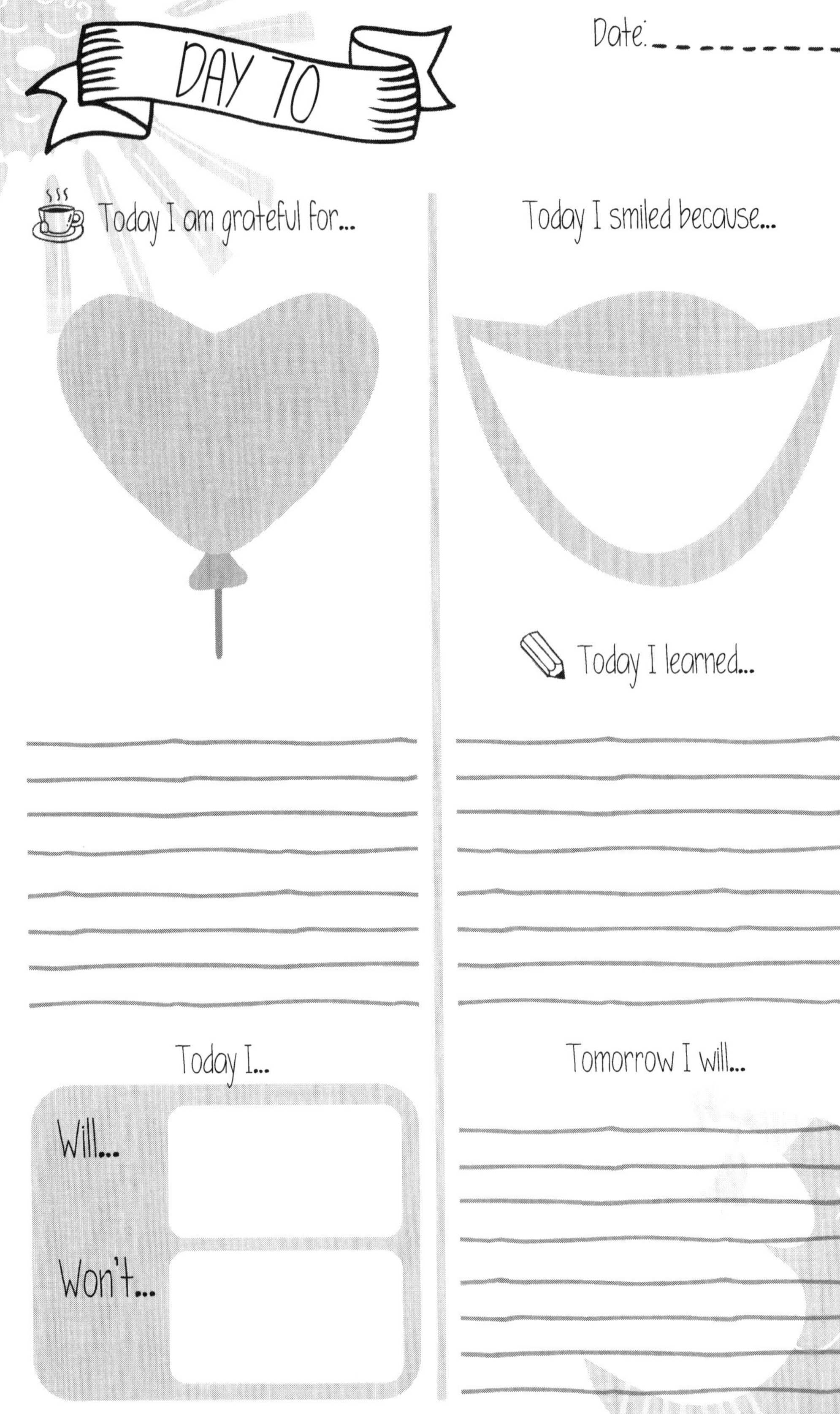

DAY 70

Date: __________

Today I am grateful for...

Today I smiled because...

Today I learned...

Today I...

Will...

Won't...

Tomorrow I will...

Week 10 In Review

Date: ____________

Things that have gone well...

Things that could have been better...

Things I learned about myself...

Next week I will...

DAY 71

Date: __________

Today I am grateful for...

Today I smiled because...

Today I learned...

Today I...

Will...

Won't...

Tomorrow I will...

Date: __________

Today I am grateful for...

Today I smiled because...

Today I learned...

Today I...

Will...

Won't...

Tomorrow I will...

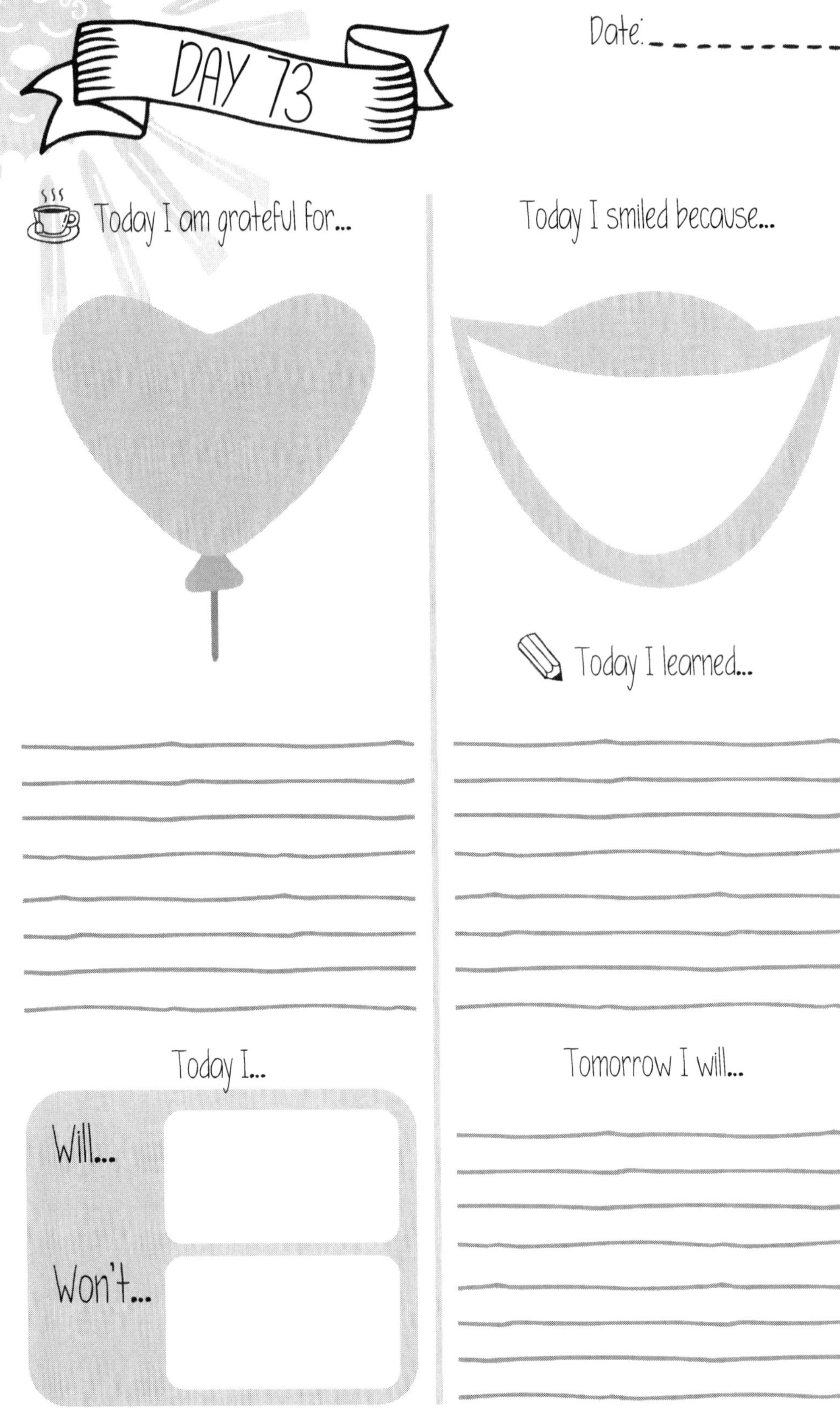

DAY 73
Date:
Today I am grateful for...
Today I smiled because...
Today I learned...
Today I...
Will...
Won't...
Tomorrow I will...

DAY 74

Date: __________

Today I am grateful for...

Today I smiled because...

Today I learned...

Today I...

Will...

Won't...

Tomorrow I will...

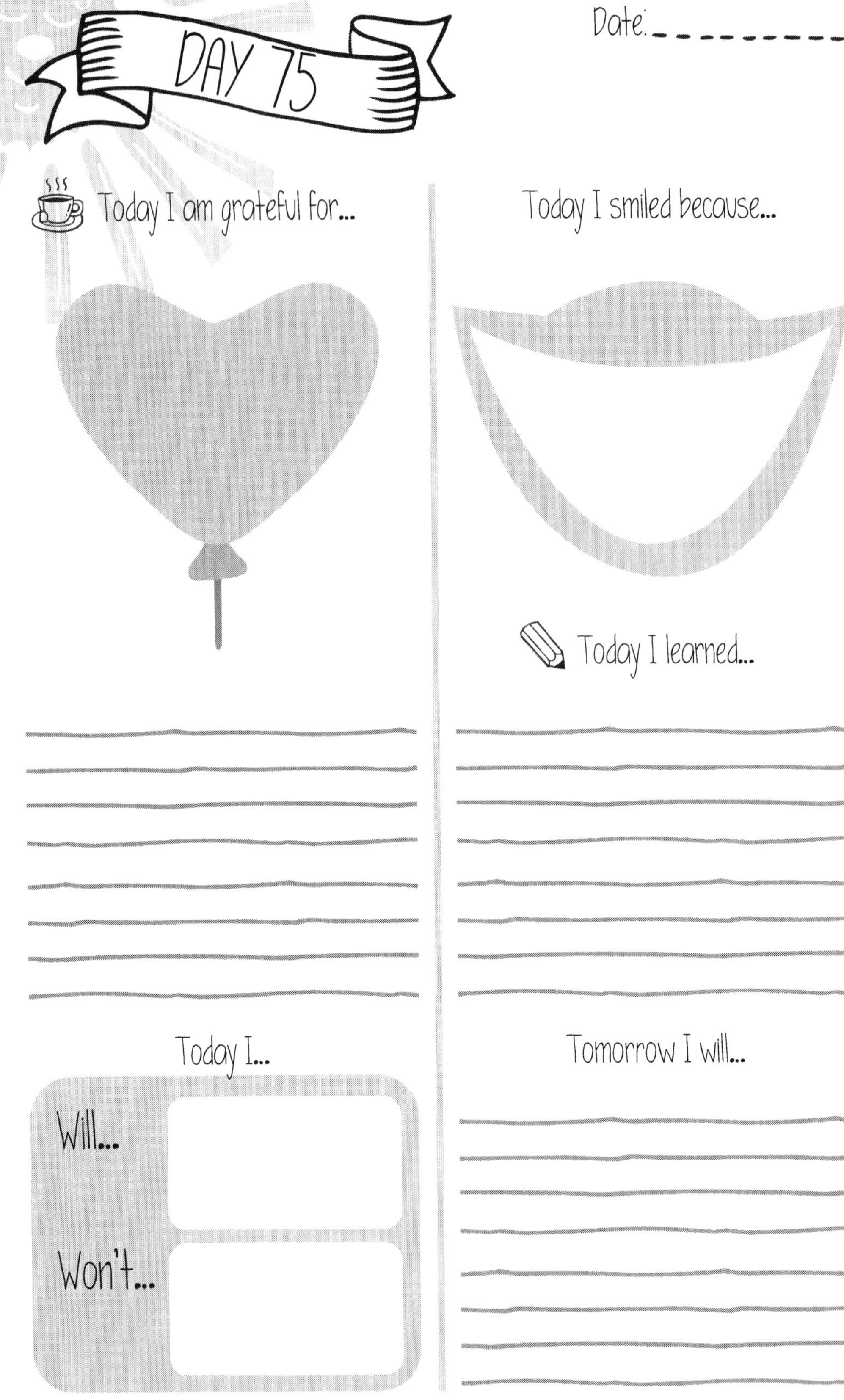

DAY 75
Date:
Today I am grateful for...
Today I smiled because...
Today I learned...
Today I...
Will...
Won't...
Tomorrow I will...

DAY 76
Date:
Today I am grateful for...
Today I smiled because...
Today I learned...
Today I...
Will...
Won't...
Tomorrow I will...

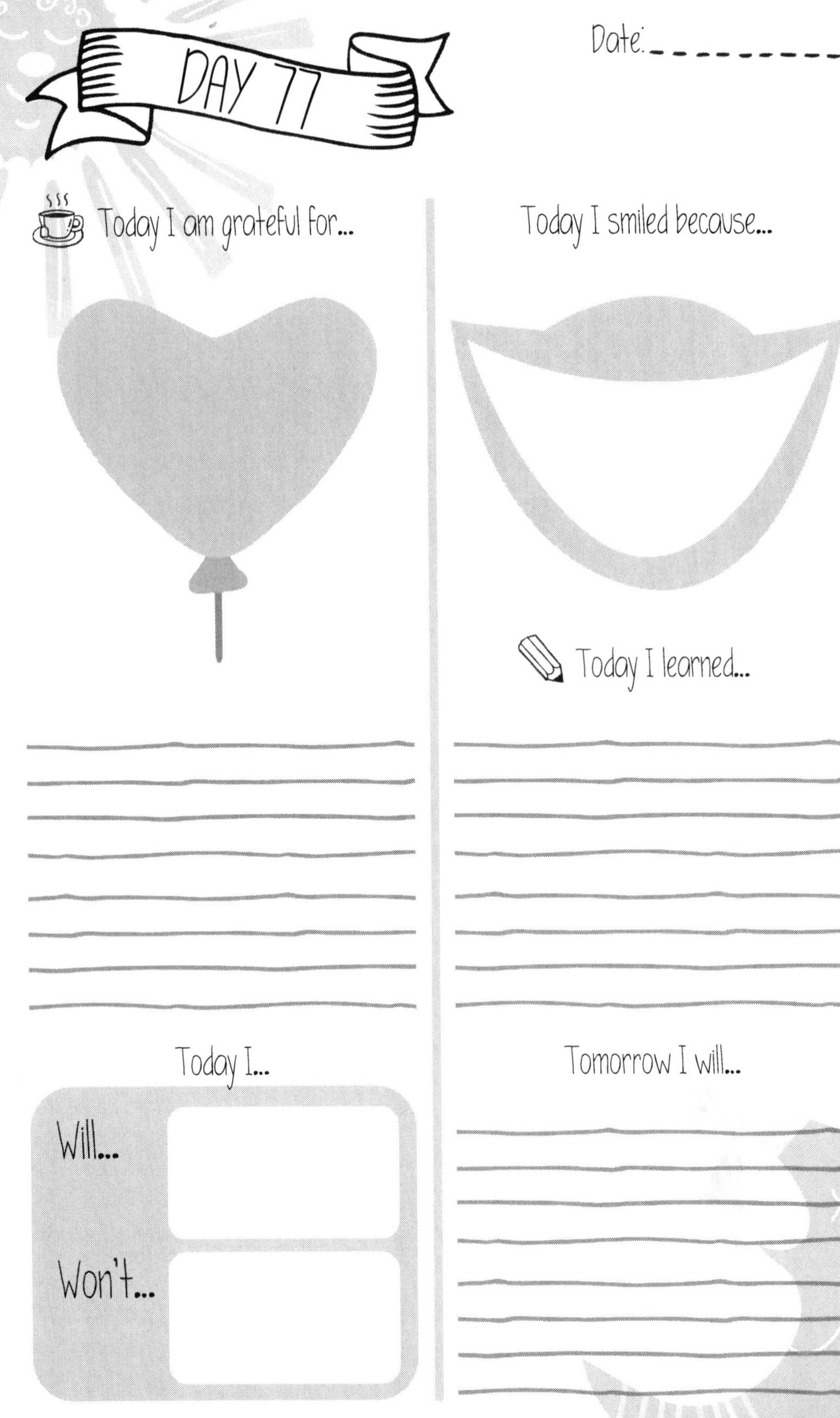
DAY 77
Date:
Today I am grateful for...
Today I smiled because...
Today I learned...
Today I...
Will...
Won't...
Tomorrow I will...

Week 11 In Review

Date: ____________

Things that have gone well...

Things that could have been better...

Things I learned about myself...

Next week I will...

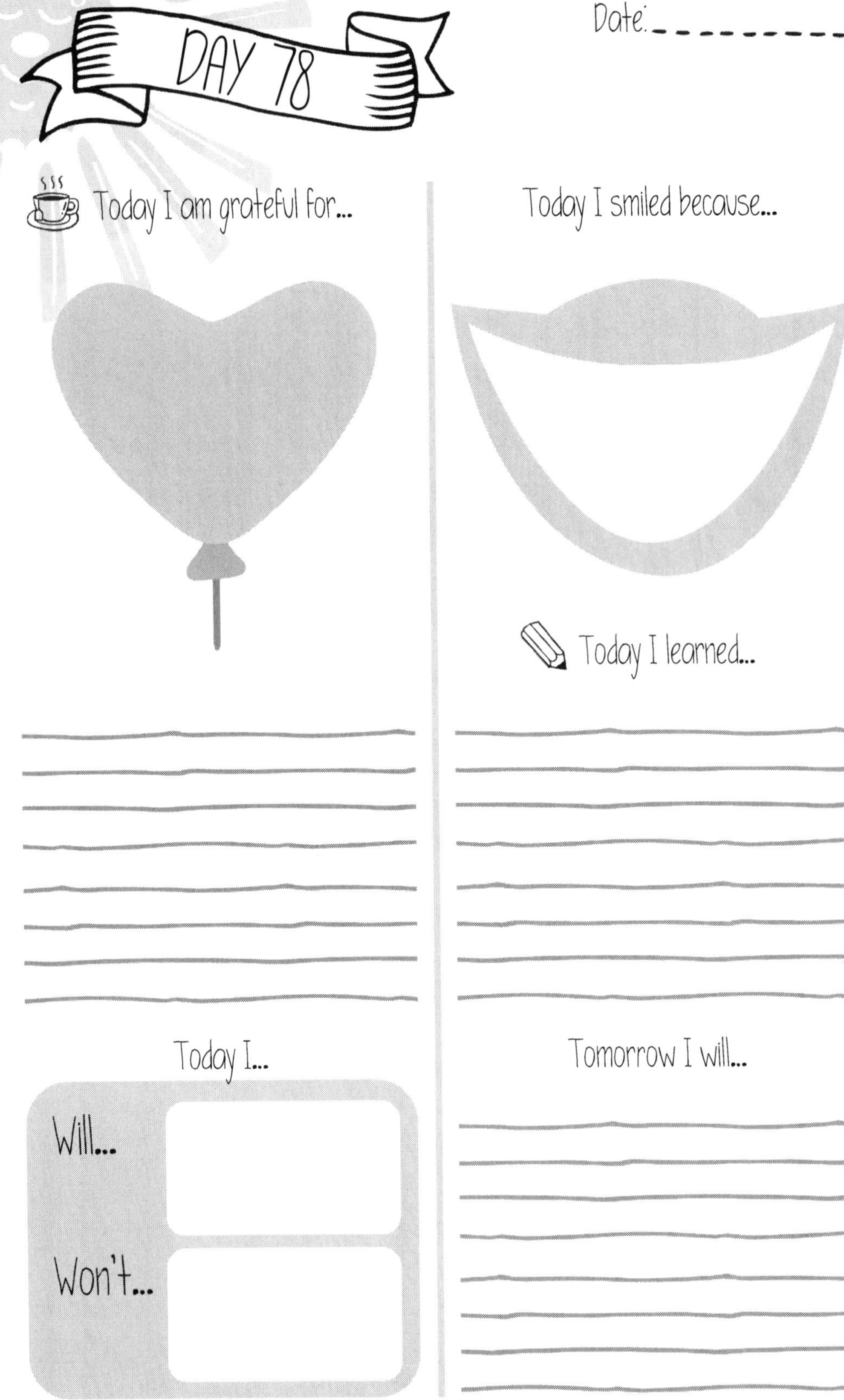
DAY 78
Date:
Today I am grateful for...
Today I smiled because...
Today I learned...
Today I...
Will...
Won't...
Tomorrow I will...

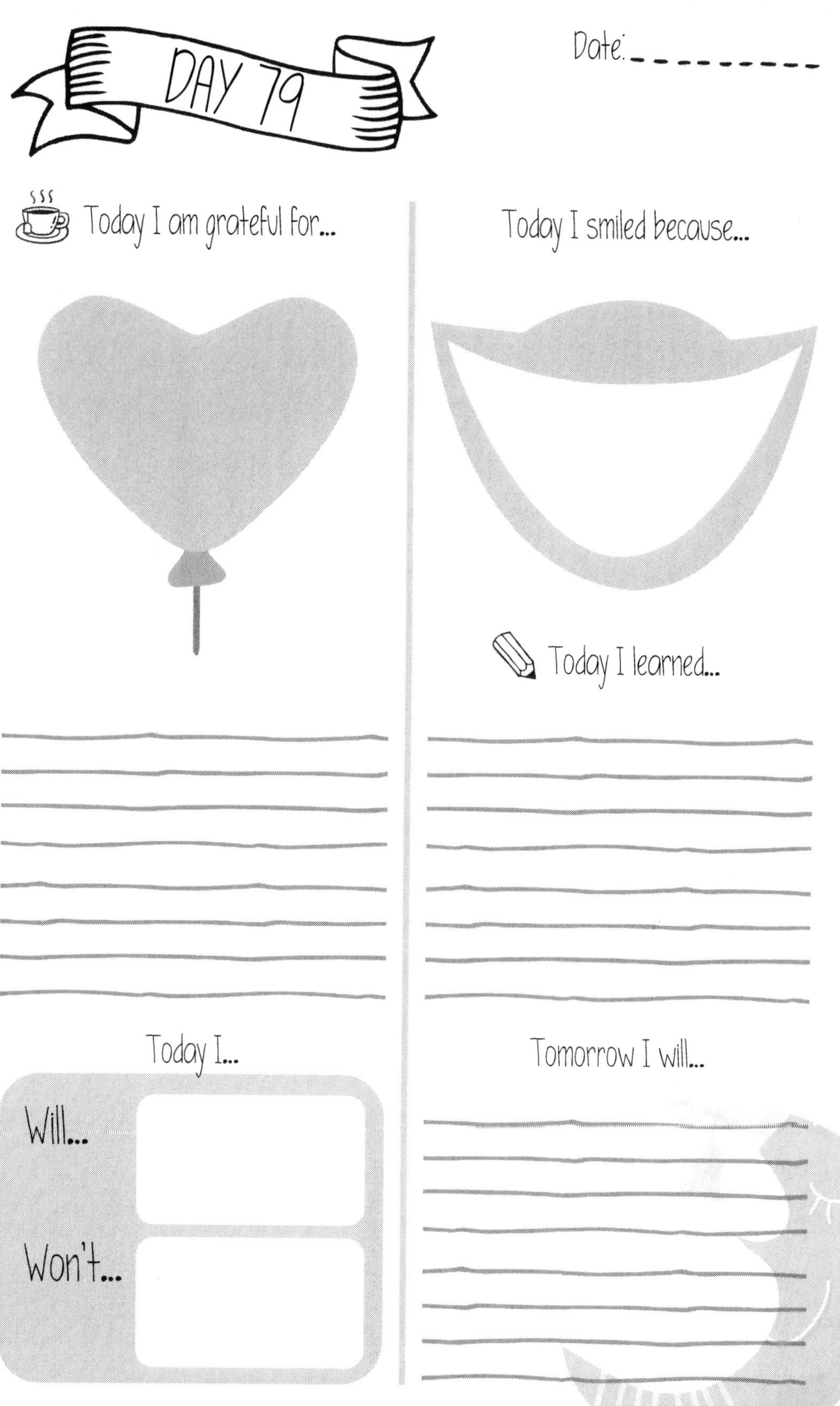
DAY 79
Date:
Today I am grateful for...
Today I smiled because...
Today I learned...
Today I...
Will...
Won't...
Tomorrow I will...

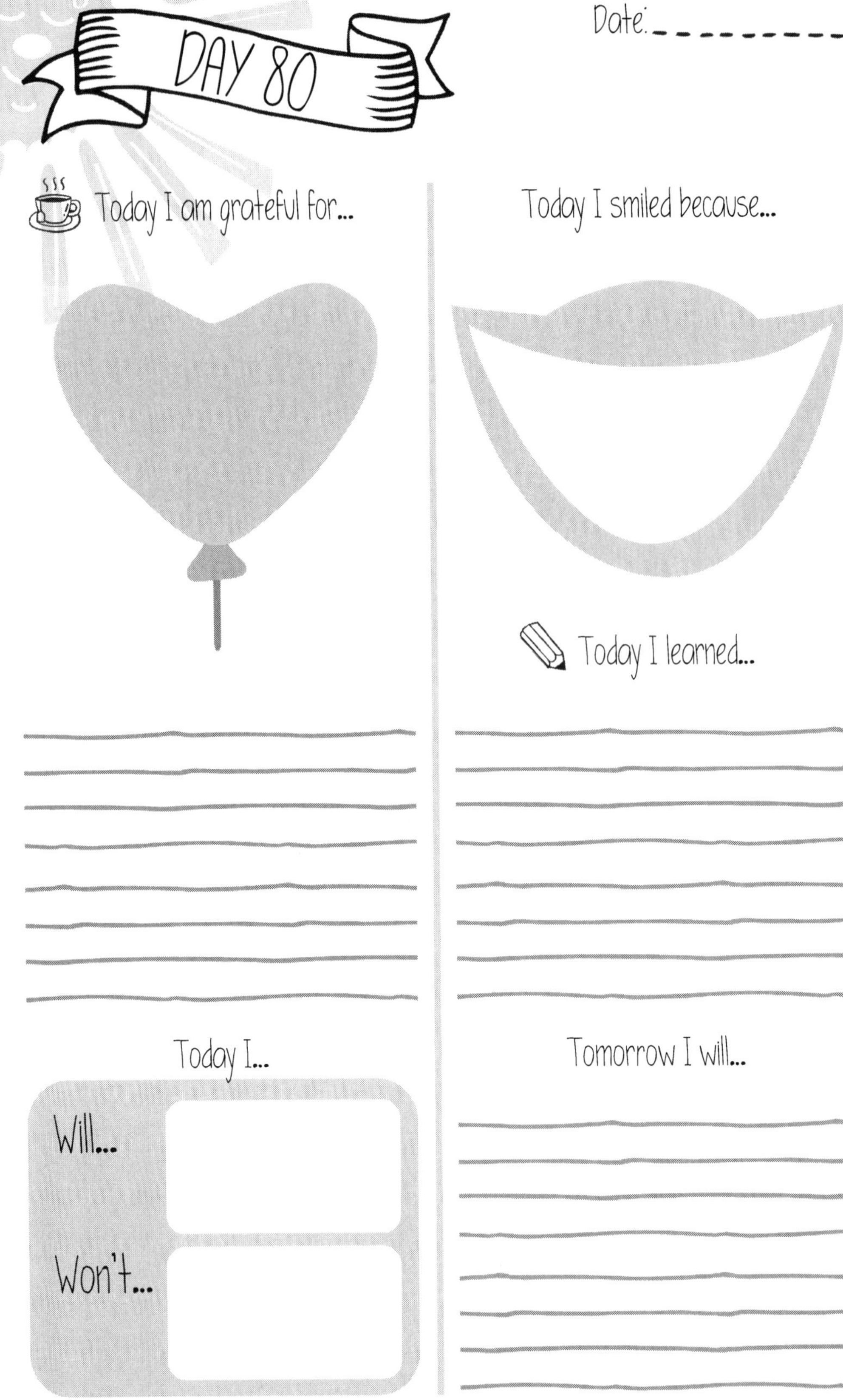
DAY 80
Date:
Today I am grateful for...
Today I smiled because...
Today I learned...
Today I...
Will...
Won't...
Tomorrow I will...

DAY 81

Date: __________

Today I am grateful for...

Today I smiled because...

Today I learned...

Today I...

Will...

Won't...

Tomorrow I will...

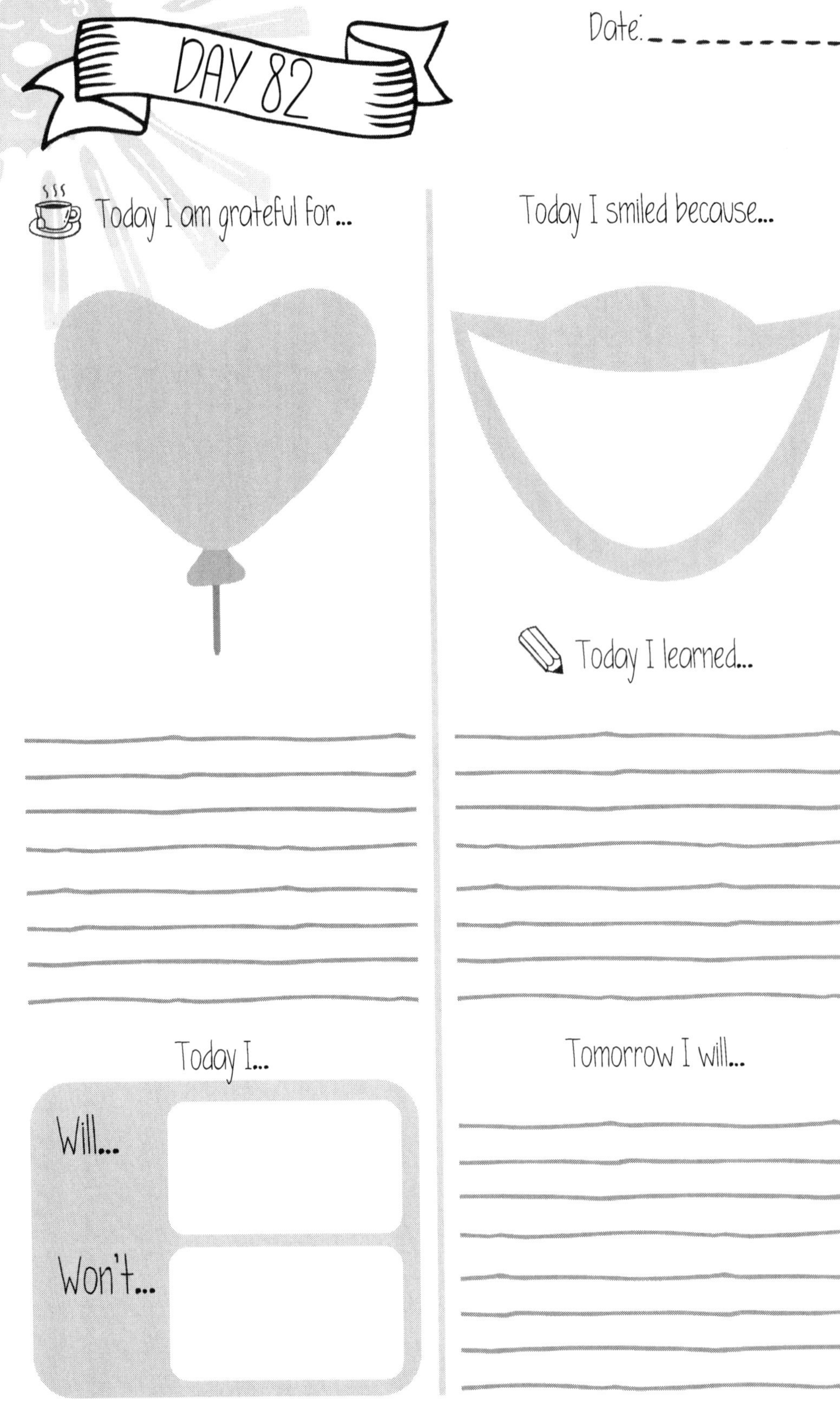
DAY 82
Date:
Today I am grateful for...
Today I smiled because...
Today I learned...
Today I...
Will...
Won't...
Tomorrow I will...

Date: __________

Today I am grateful for...

Today I smiled because...

Today I learned...

Today I...

Will...

Won't...

Tomorrow I will...

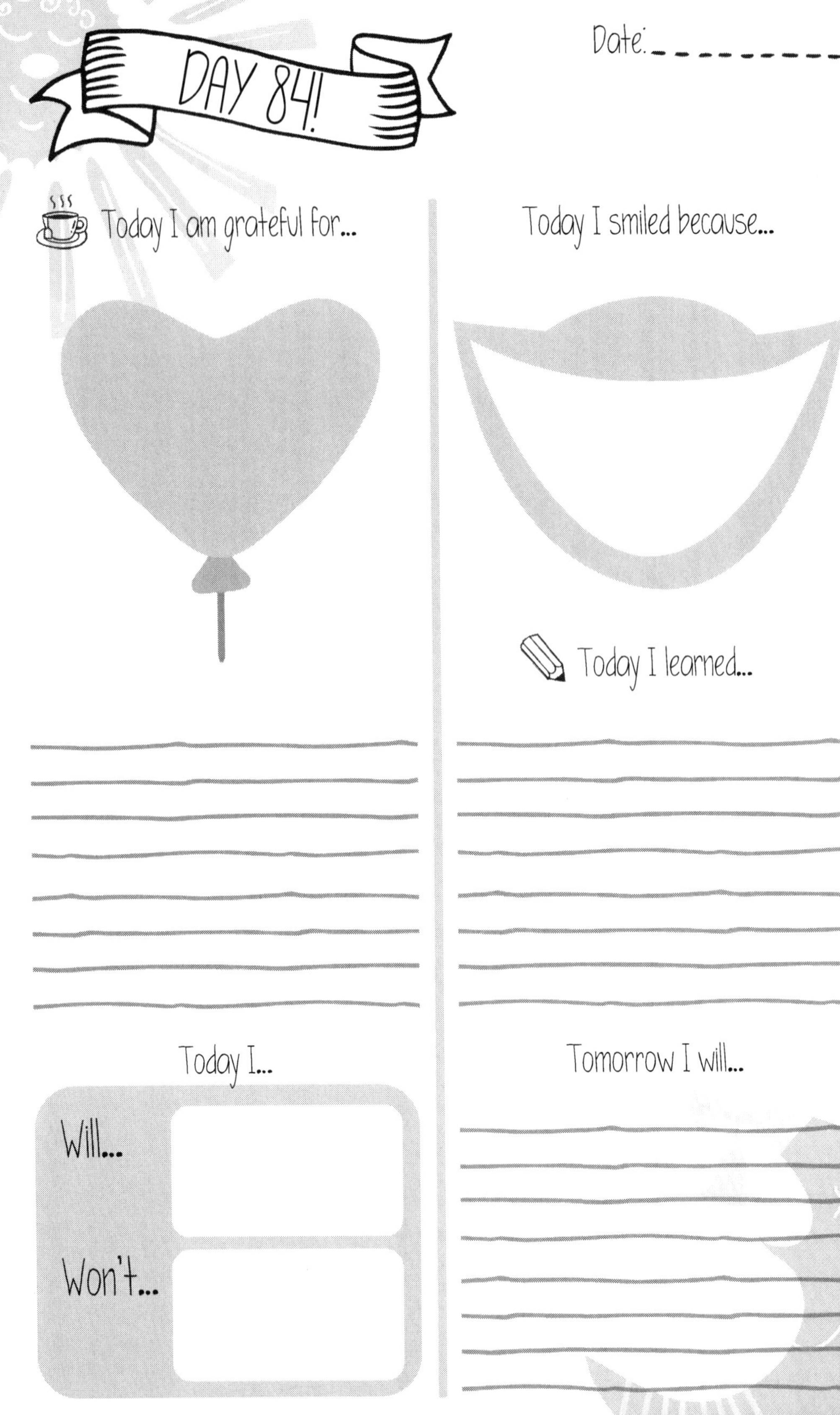

DAY 84!

Date: __________

Today I am grateful for...

Today I smiled because...

Today I learned...

Today I...

Will...

Won't...

Tomorrow I will...

Week 12 In Review!

Date: ___________

Things that have gone well...

Things that could have been better...

Things I learned about myself...

Next week I will...

“The best way to
predict your future
is to create it.”

Abraham Lincoln

Whoosh! Was that the finishing line you just ran past?!

If you've managed to complete the whole twelve weeks of your journey to a new sober you, **huge congratulations!** You should be feeling incredibly proud!

This is the start of a great adventure. A new, sober, life where you – not alcohol – are in control. Hopefully by now you are realising the massive benefits of being sober and seeing positive changes in your life. It keeps getting better, believe me!

"I didn't quite make it... what do I do now?"

If you haven't managed a completely sober twelve weeks, don't stress yourself over it too much. Yes, it would be better if you had – no one is going to pretend otherwise. We shouldn't be in the business of self-delusion – that's alcohol's trick to play, not ours.

We need to be honest with ourselves if we are to succeed. What matters is you've tried, and you've learned a lot about yourself, your drinking habits and your triggers. This will make it easier next time around.

When it comes to stopping drinking, there really is no time like the present. Continue to use the rest of the journal and work to improve day-by-day, then start a new journal. But keep this one as a reminder of what happened this time.

Compare your days and look for signs of improvement or for things you could have done differently. Make sure you get involved in groups like the *Alcohol-Free Community*. Speak to your doctor or alcohol services if you feel the need. Most importantly, never, ever, feel alone.

Going forward to 100 days

Yes, the title of this book is *12 Weeks To A Sober Life* but isn't 100 a nice round number? As a bonus, journal for another 16 days and then reward yourself with something special!

ONWARDS AND UPWARDS TO 100!

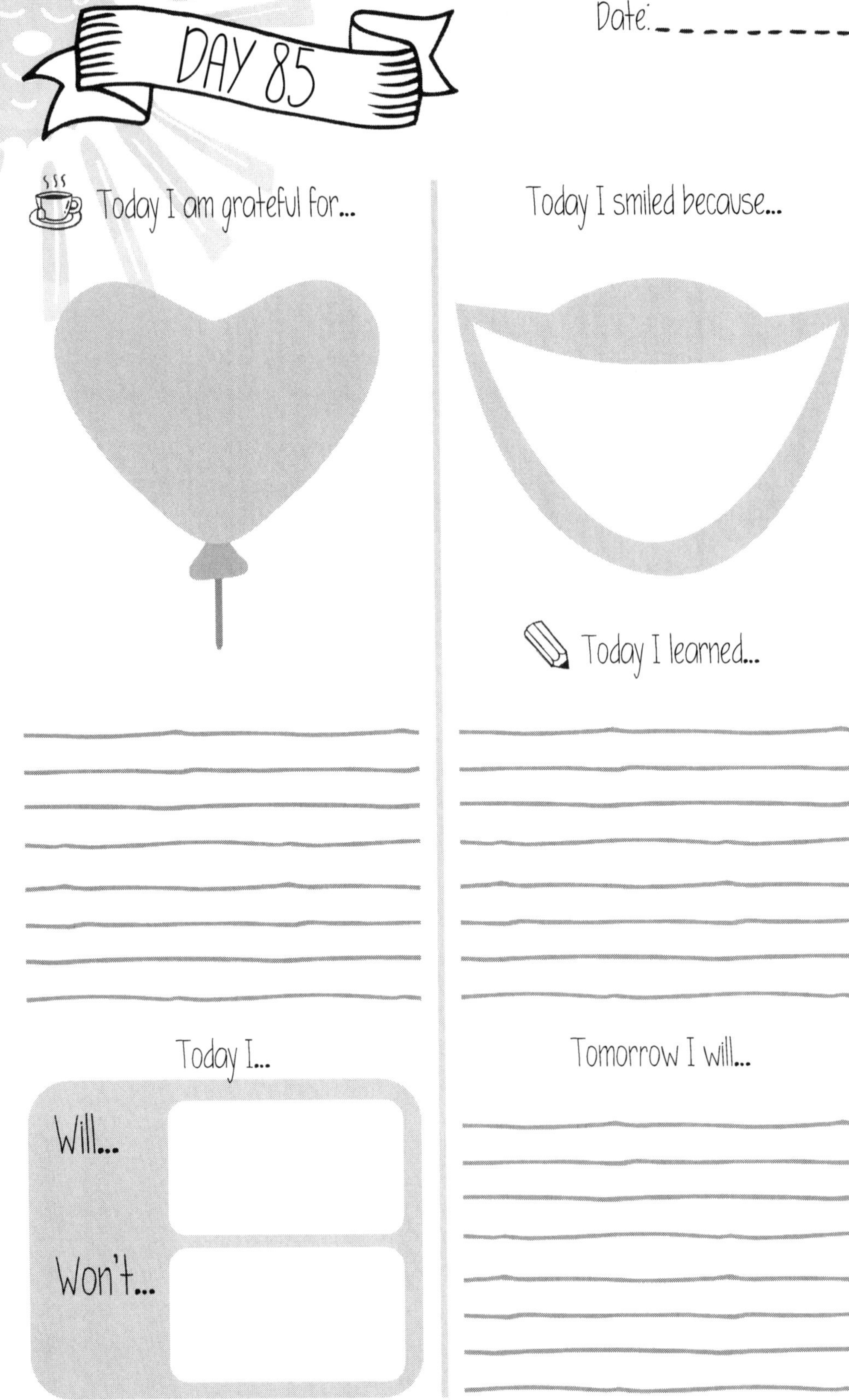
DAY 85
Date:
Today I am grateful for...
Today I smiled because...
Today I learned...
Today I...
Will...
Won't...
Tomorrow I will...

Date: ___________

Today I am grateful for...

Today I smiled because...

Today I learned...

Today I...

Will...

Won't...

Tomorrow I will...

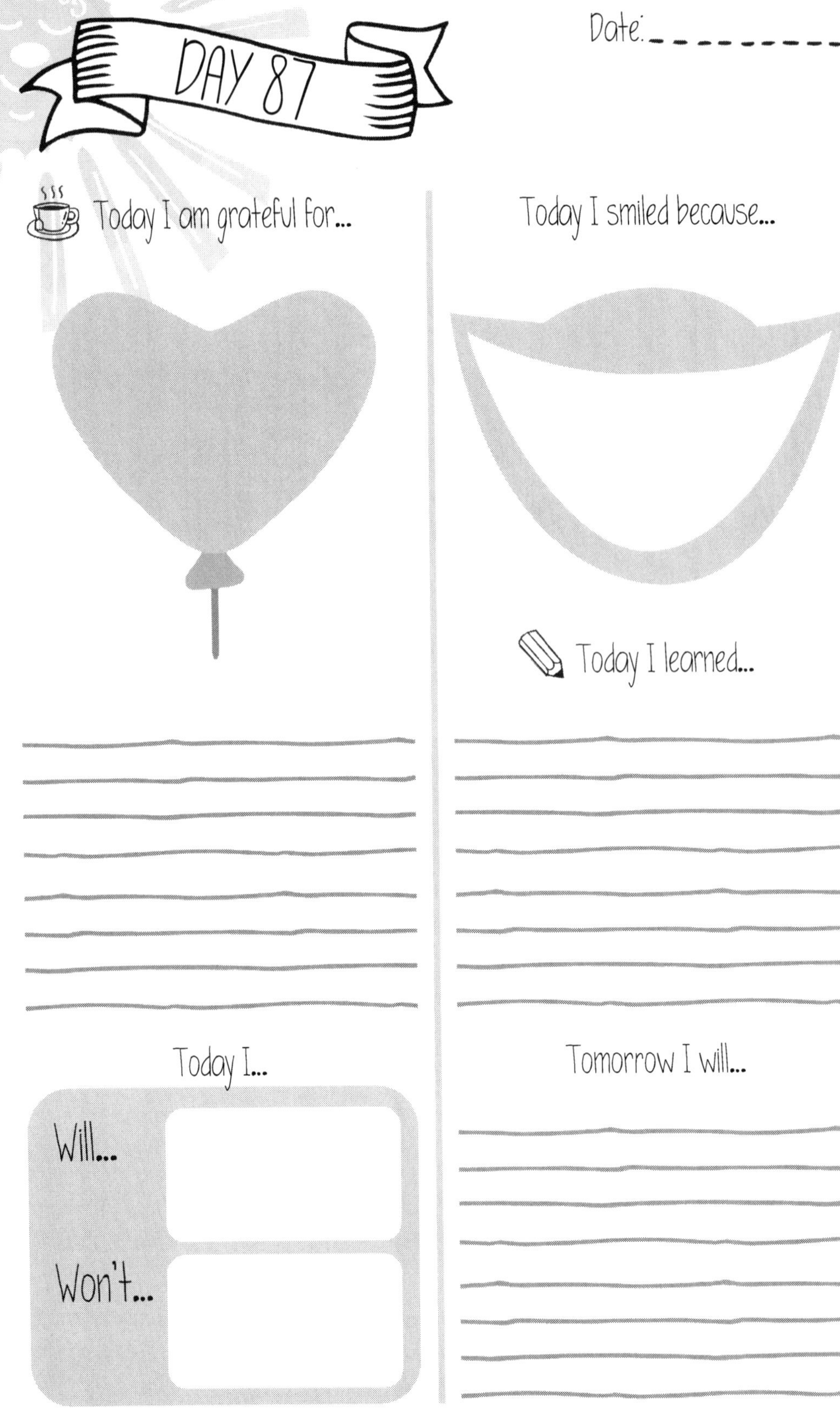
DAY 87
Date:
Today I am grateful for...
Today I smiled because...
Today I learned...
Today I...
Will...
Won't...
Tomorrow I will...

Date: ___________

Today I am grateful for...

Today I smiled because...

Today I learned...

Today I...

Will...

Won't...

Tomorrow I will...

DAY 89

Date:_________

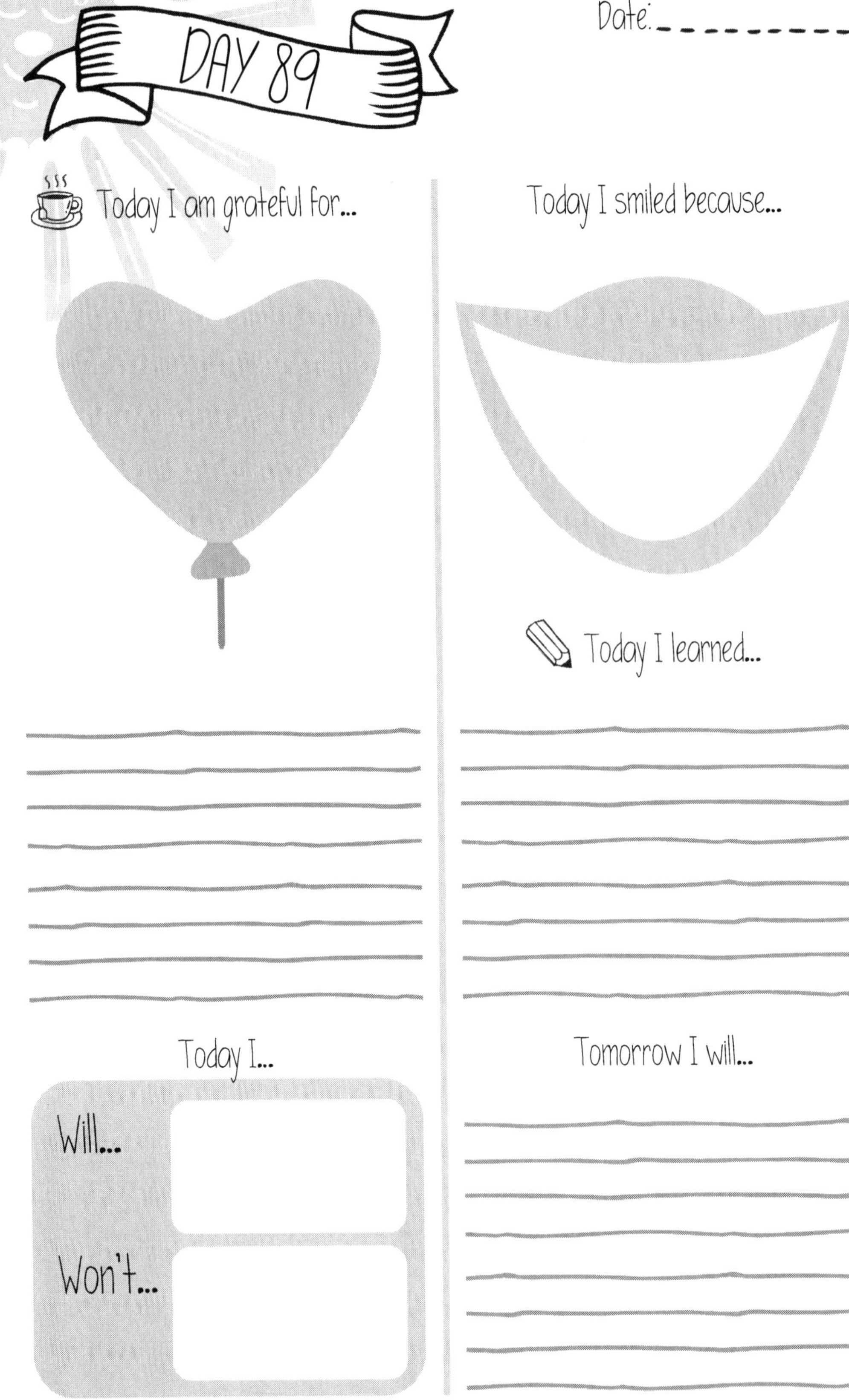

Today I am grateful for...

Today I smiled because...

Today I learned...

Today I...

Will...

Won't...

Tomorrow I will...

Date:

Today I am grateful for...

Today I smiled because...

Today I learned...

Today I...

Will...

Won't...

Tomorrow I will...

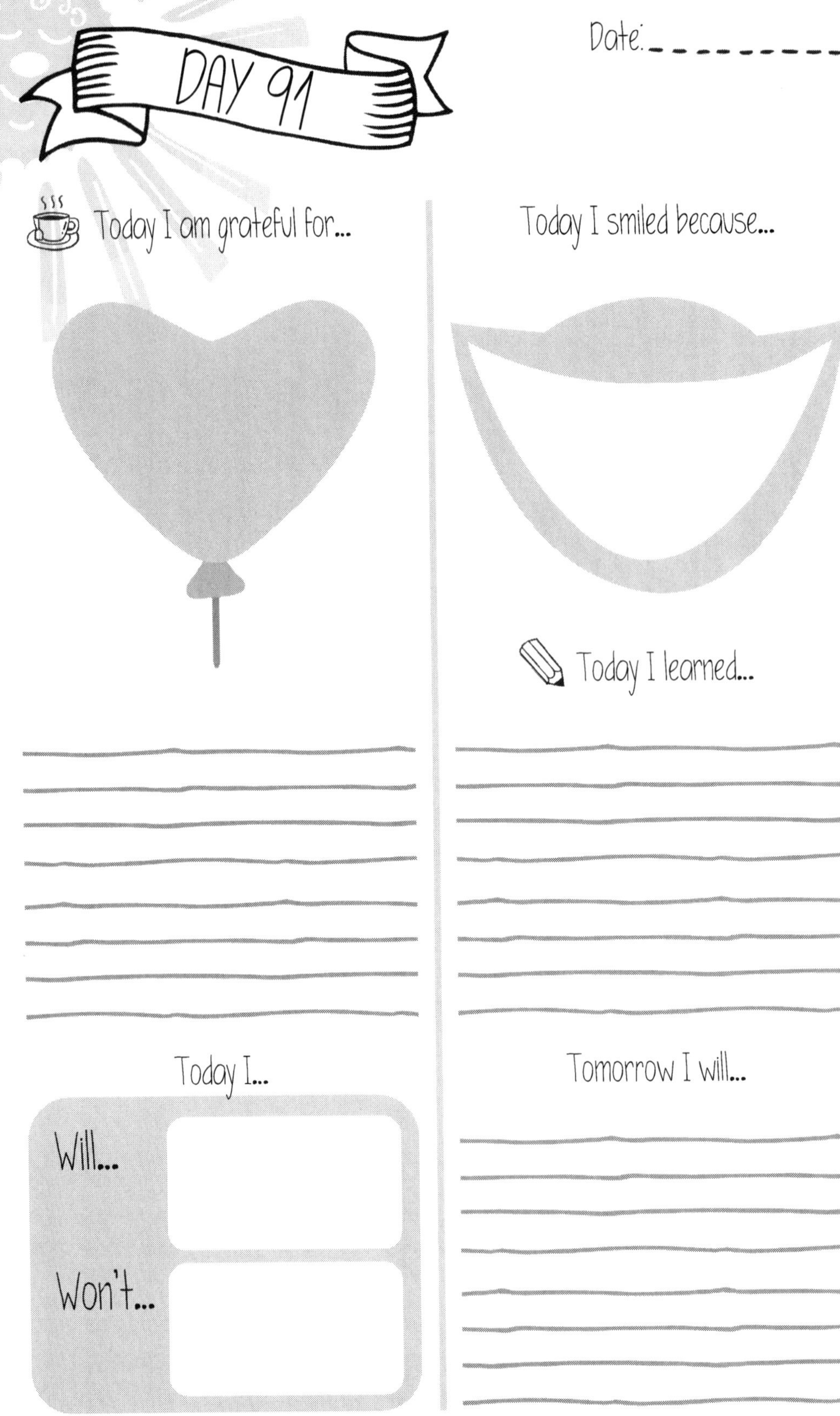
DAY 91
Date:
Today I am grateful for...
Today I smiled because...
Today I learned...
Today I...
Will...
Won't...
Tomorrow I will...

Date: __________

Today I am grateful for...

Today I learned...

Today I...

Will...

Won't...

Tomorrow I will...

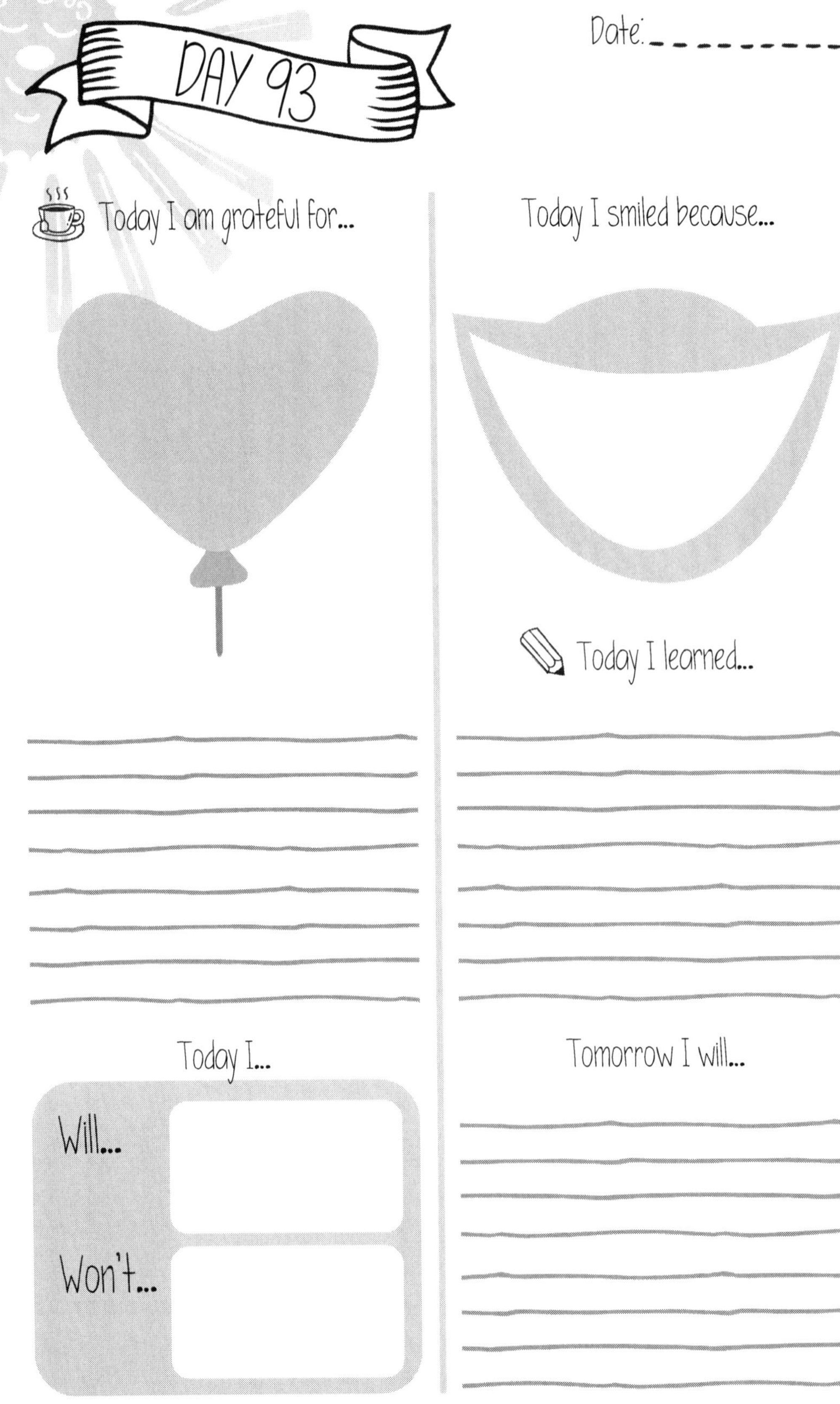
DAY 93
Date:
Today I am grateful for...
Today I smiled because...
Today I learned...
Today I...
Will...
Won't...
Tomorrow I will...

DAY 94

Date: __________

Today I am grateful for...

Today I smiled because...

Today I learned...

Today I...

Will...

Won't...

Tomorrow I will...

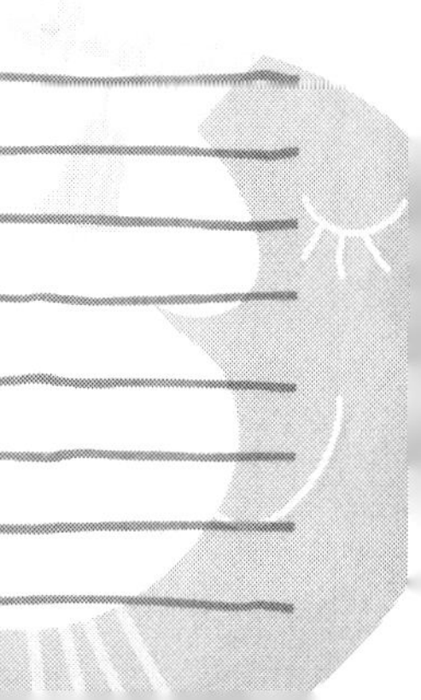

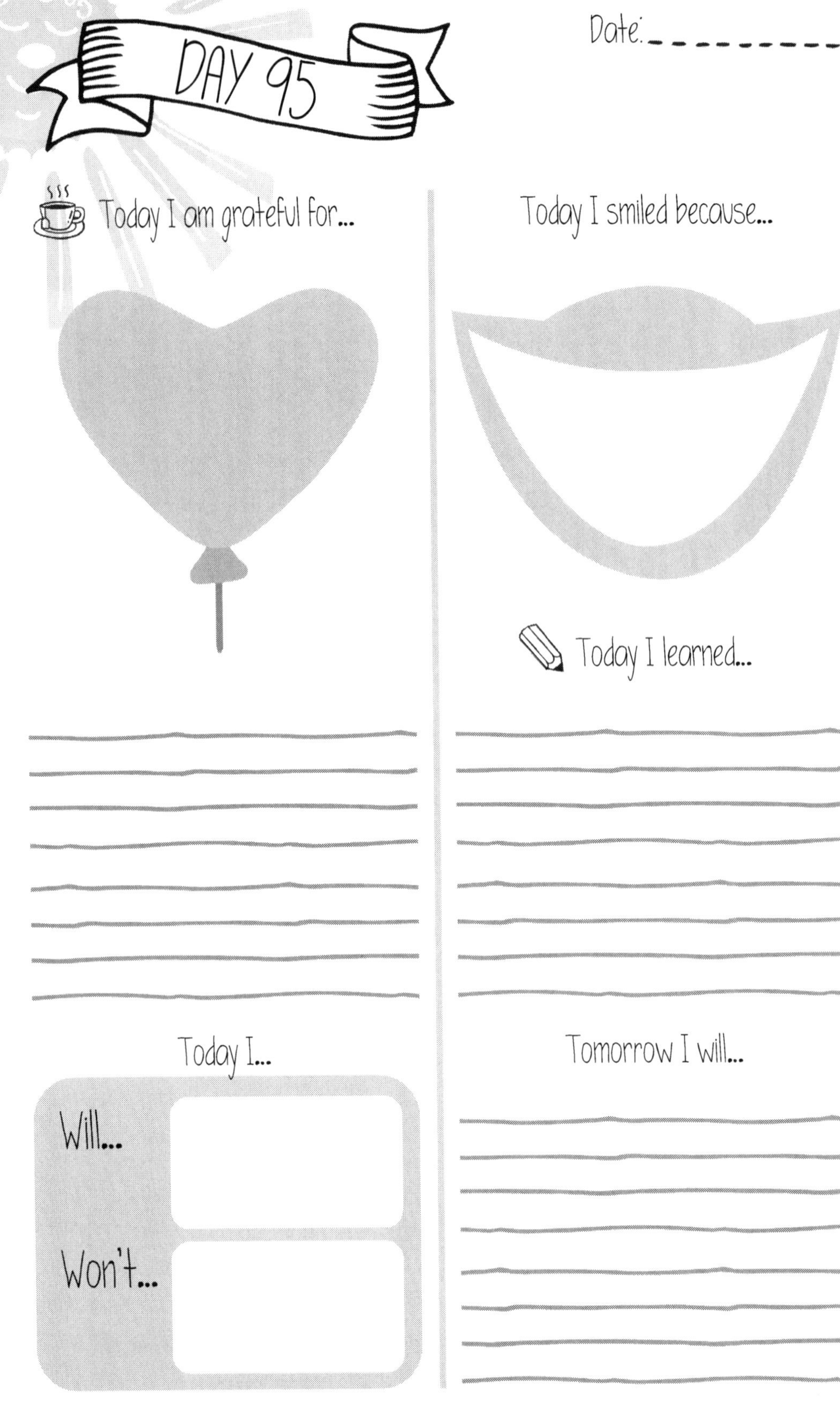
DAY 95
Date:
Today I am grateful for...
Today I smiled because...
Today I learned...
Today I...
Will...
Won't...
Tomorrow I will...

Date: __________

Today I learned...

Today I...

Will...

Won't...

Tomorrow I will...

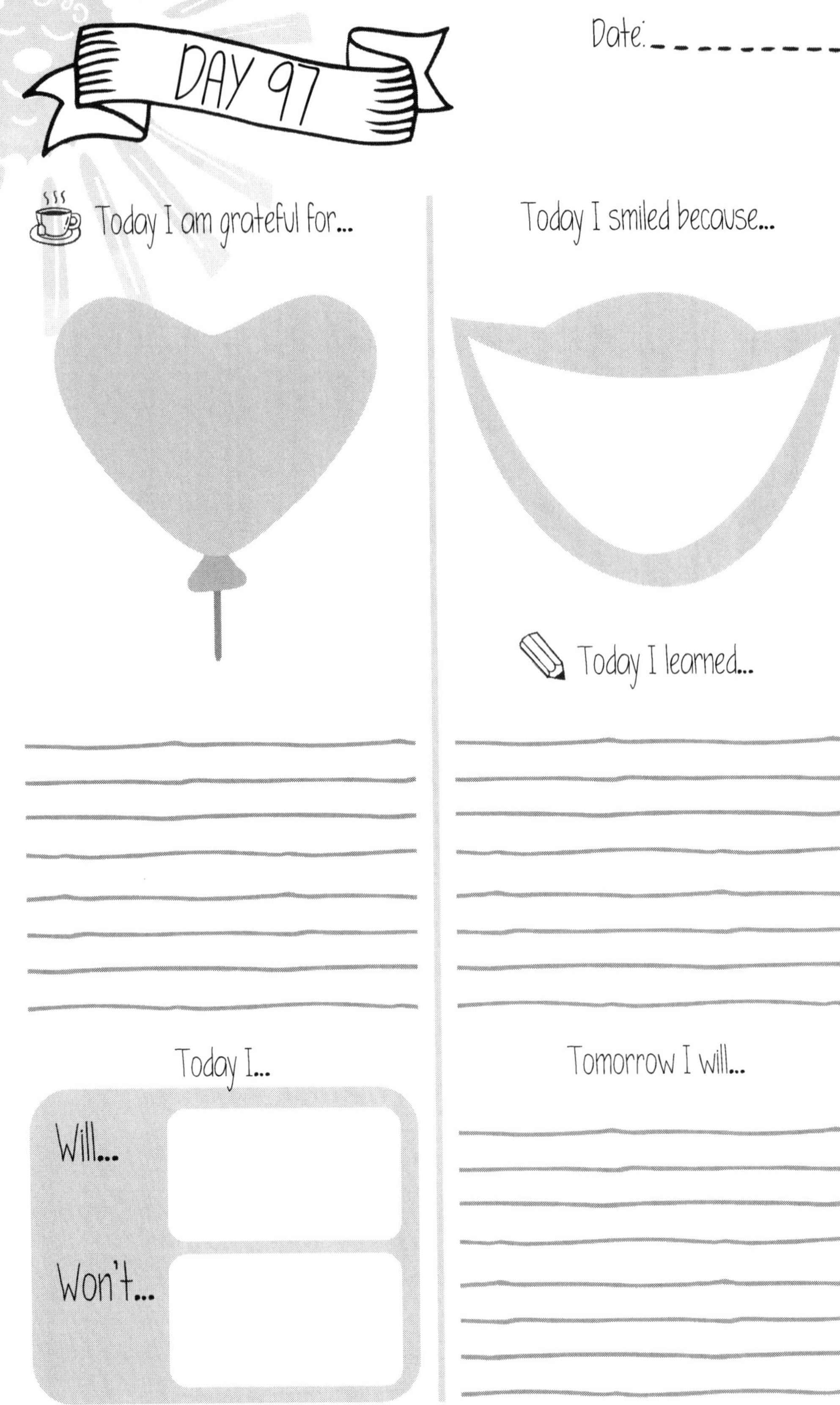
DAY 97
Date:
Today I am grateful for...
Today I smiled because...
Today I learned...
Today I...
Will...
Won't...
Tomorrow I will...

Date:

Today I am grateful for...

Today I smiled because...

Today I learned...

Today I...

Will...

Won't...

Tomorrow I will...

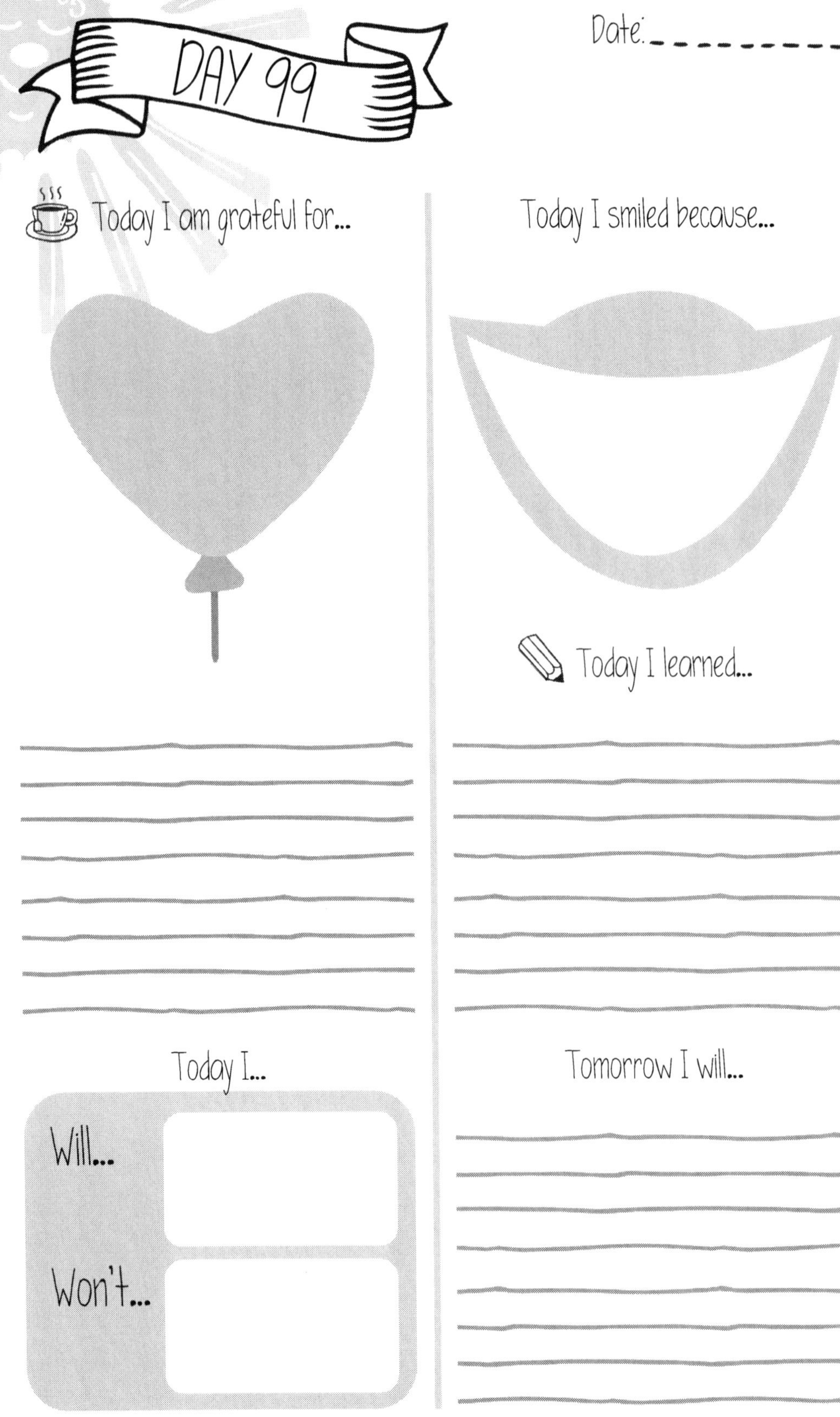
DAY 99
Date:
Today I am grateful for...
Today I smiled because...
Today I learned...
Today I...
Will...
Won't...
Tomorrow I will...

Date: __________

Today I am grateful for...

Today I smiled because...

Today I learned...

Today I...

Will...

Won't...

Tomorrow I will...

100 Days In Review!

Date: ___________

Things that have gone well...

Things that could have been better...

Things I learned about myself...

Next week I will...

You've done something truly special!

Whether or not you managed to complete the whole 100 days without alcohol, you've achieved something incredible by completing this journal.

By now you should know more about yourself and your drinking than you ever have, and you're on the path to a lifetime of sobriety and recovery!

Did you complete all 100 days?

If you have managed to complete the 100 days sober, continue doing what you're doing! You've already gained a lot; freedom from the daily grip of alcohol, improved health, more time, increased self-respect, and so much more.

And this is just the start. Stay sober, stay healthy, keep busy, and make sure you keep journaling. But most of all, enjoy your new life!

Still got a bit more work to do?

If you've not quite managed 100 straight days sober, don't worry. You've still gained so much from this experience and you can now build on that.

Make sure you read through your journal from the start and look for patterns or reasons why you weren't able to complete the 100 days unbroken.

You've still done great work in recording your journey so far, and this will be a vital help for your next attempt. Good luck, you can do this!

START ANOTHER JOURNAL AND BELIEVE IN YOURSELF! xx

Wishing you continued success,

“The only real mistake is the one from which we learn nothing.”

Henry Ford

Thank you for reading – and using – *12 Weeks To A Sober Life*. We hope you've found it helpful in your journey to a new life.

If you have enjoyed this book, please visit the web site you bought it from and leave an honest review.

This will help other people find the book and help them in their journey to a sober life.

To be informed of new books by Alcohol-Free Press, please join our mailing list by sending an email to join@alcoholfree.press

You can unsubscribe at any time and all details are fully confidential.

Thank you!

Printed in Great Britain
by Amazon